# The Collector's Book of
# ART NOUVEAU

# BOOKS BY MARIAN KLAMKIN

Flower Arranging for Period Decoration

Flower Arrangements That Last

The Collector's Book of Art Nouveau

The Collector's Book of Bottles

The Collector's Book of Boxes

The Collector's Book of Wedgwood

*Frontispiece*

RIGHT *Porcelain vase made by Rozenberg of the Hague*
LEFT *Poster, Eugène Grasset*

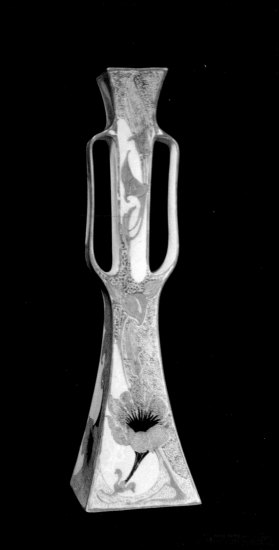

The Collector's Book of
# ART NOUVEAU

## MARIAN KLAMKIN

Illustrated with photographs by Charles Klamkin

**DODD, MEAD & COMPANY · NEW YORK**

First published in the United States in 1971

All rights reserved

ISBN 0 - 396 - 06367 - 5

Library of Congress Catalog Card Number: 74 - 154064

Printed in Great Britain

# Contents

*The author wishes to express her thanks to the Victoria & Albert Museum, London, for allowing her to reproduce photographs of their exhibits.*

# I
# Introduction

Towards the end of the nineteenth century an art movement that seemed totally original in concept and execution was developed. This movement, starting in England, became truly international. It brought talented young artists into the design of the decorative and graphic arts. Thought to be inconsequential and tasteless by the Victorians, the Art Nouveau movement still influences our modern taste in home decorating and many other areas of the applied arts. For the first time in the history of the decorative arts there were simultaneous movements in England, France, Germany and other countries of Europe and, to a lesser degree, in America, to bring together the finest designers and craftsmen in order to unify the designs of buildings, furniture, wallpapers, fabrics, ceramics, metalwork and glass. The common aim of these groups of artists was to integrate the useful with the beautiful in the highest artistic manner.

Art Nouveau was more than a style; it was a philosophy. From this philosophy came a renaissance of carefully made and thoughtfully designed articles for the home, each intended to fit into the scheme of the whole. Line became the most important aspect of Art Nouveau design and the importance of shape and texture of an object replaced the over-decoration of the Victorian period and marked the beginning of the emphasis in design of the functionalists who followed.

It is questionable whether we are yet fully aware of the influence that this widespread movement in the applied arts has had on the designs that followed. The Art Nouveau movement was a rebellion of the artists against the machine-made articles of the nineteenth century that were copies or adaptations of past designs. However, the Art Nouveau designers also borrowed from the past. Eventually, the machines produced articles in Art Nouveau style and some of the

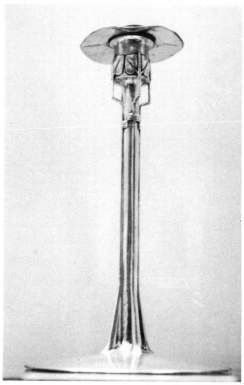

*(above) Candlestick, silver. Hand-raised, from a design by R. C. Silver. Illustrated in* The Studio, *Vol XIX, 1900. Birmingham hallmarked for 1906-7. [Victoria and Albert Museum]; (right) Tiffany peacock vase. Blue iridescent colour with peacock tail feather motif. Signed: Louis C. Tiffany. [John Jesse]*

results were quite successful artistically.

Because of the emphasis on line and the adaptation of natural forms to design, Art Nouveau is easily distinguishable from any other period in the decorative arts. Collectors have been buying the best known work of this period for the past fifteen years and those who are aware of the world of decorative arts are familiar with the work of Louis Comfort Tiffany of America, Emile Gallé of France, and the many innovative British artists and designers who were responsible for the development of Art Nouveau as a style. Museums all over the world have been foresighted enough to preserve not only their best national examples of Art Nouveau but those works of other countries that are considered to have been innovative and to have influenced the work done in this short but important period.

Fortunately, because of the principle of Art Nouveau that many good artists should be gathered together to work on one project, there were, considering the short period of time this style was thought to have lasted, a large number of items produced and marketed. The most collectable are the early innovative hand-made items of the late 1890s. Glassware, ceramics, furniture and metal items are available for the knowledgeable collector. Those items, such as the glassware of Tiffany, that were high-priced when they were first made, and then later could not be given away, are again expensive.

However, there are many items of the Art Nouveau period less well known than Tiffany glass that will be of equal value someday, that are not recognised by any but the most knowledgeable of collectors and that may still be found if the collector is in the right place at the right time. Even the later machine-made articles are becoming collectable. In other words, many items of the Art Nouveau period are the valuable antiques of the future. Once a collector can forget about 'age snobbery' and is able to convince himself that investment in articles that are less than 100 years old is worthwhile, he will be able to collect articles of first rate design and execution that can only increase in value as time goes on.

Although glass made at the turn of the century has appeared to be the most desirable medium for collecting so far, it is by no means the only one. Because important and talented artists turned to the decorative arts as they had never done before in order to create interiors that were totally of the 'new style', there are books, posters, ceramics, silver, ironware, pewter, furniture and many other articles that are all important in the history of the decorative arts. One exciting aspect of collecting Art Nouveau is that all the best items have not yet found their way into museums, and the knowledgeable collector can still find excellent examples. There are still good items to be found at estate auctions and secondhand stores. Those antique dealers who pride themselves on the age of their wares do not usually buy nor deal in articles of this period, so the bidding at auctions is often less active for articles of Art Nouveau than it is for older collectables.

The man who is interested in the Art Nouveau period has many things to learn before he starts to collect. There are many areas where research and knowledge can lead him to some of the few bargains to be found in collecting for the home. The field of Art Nouveau collecting is, on the whole, safer as an investment than just about any other period in the applied arts. Because the style lasted a comparatively short time and was not universally popular even at its peak, there have been few attempts to copy the many items that were made. Art Nouveau furniture prices have not yet soared so high that it pays a cabinetmaker to copy the designs. It may be comforting to the collector to know that when he buys an Art Nouveau desk or table that the brasses are probably original and that the entire piece is 'of the period'. There are still many treasures awaiting discovery.

It is the purpose of this book to point out the characteristics of items made during this artistic period in the decorative arts, and to bring light to bear on those carefully designed and made articles that many of our parents scorned but which are today recognised as being of good design and of historic importance in the field of the decorative arts. Since the style manifested itself somewhat differently in different countries the national characteristics of Art Nouveau design will be discussed also. This should be of some help in identifying many of the unmarked hand-made articles which the collector will come upon from time to time.

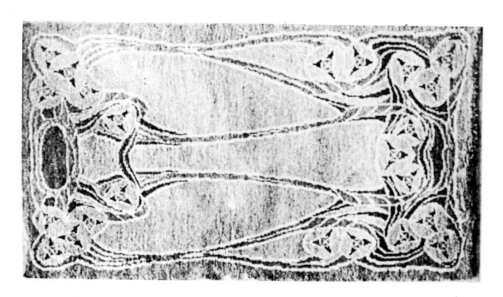

*Rug, French. Designed and excuted by Maurice Dufresne. Illustrated in* The Studio Yearbook of Decorative Art *for 1908.*

# 2
# Influences and Background
# of Art Nouveau

It is not our purpose here to go into a scholarly dissertation on the many divergent influences—social, political, artistic and philosophical—that led to the development of an original decorative art style towards the end of the nineteenth century. However, it is necessary that the serious collector should know something of the background of Art Nouveau in order to recognise those shapes and motifs that divide Art Nouveau collectables from other decorative objects made during the latter half of the nineteenth century and the beginning of the twentieth. Since the style grew out of a particular philosophy and was an artistic movement of lasting importance, and since we have been able to view the period with better perspective than could the last generation, the interested collector can now be made aware of the important historical, artistic and philosophical influences behind the style.

The style of William Blake (1757–1827), poet and artist, exemplifies the totality of art that the later Art Nouveau artists and writers achieved. However, Blake was strongly influenced by John Flaxman, a sculptor and artist who was responsible for many of Wedgwood's neo-classic designs in jasperware. Although he was a classicist, Flaxman's drawings are closely linked to Blake's art style. Flaxman's use of bold outlines and curved lines, and his lack of detail, were adopted by Blake, who admired Flaxman greatly.

Blake's successful combination of writing and illustration, seen in his 'Songs of Innocence', was only possible because he had talents both for drawing and writing. He was a mystic, given to hallucinations, and it is this quality of mysticism that influenced the group of artists in England that became known as the Pre-Raphaelite Brotherhood. Dante Gabriel Rossetti (1828–82) was the leader of this group and he interested other

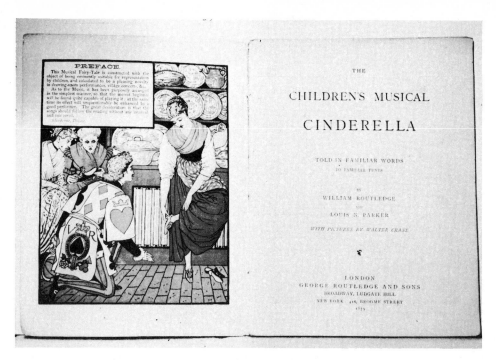

*Walter Crane used bold outlines, little shading and flat planes of colour in his illustrations for children's books. [The Christmas Tree Bookshop]*

members of the Brotherhood, among whom was Edward Burne-Jones (1833–98), in the style of Blake. The emphasis on the line as the most important aspect of a work of art is strongly apparent in Burne-Jones's earlier work.

Thus it is possible to follow the development of the Art Nouveau style through the entire nineteenth century in the aesthetic, curved, linear work of Burne-Jones, Walter Crane (1875–1915), Aubrey Beardsley (1872–98), George Heywood Sumner (1853–1940) and Herbert P. Horne (1864–1916), all of whom are considered to be Pre-Raphaelites. Rhythmic lines, flowing patterns, abstract floral designs and a preoccupation, particularly in Burne-Jones's work, with fabrics and their patterns foreshadowed the establishment in England of a distinct style embracing all decorative objects.

Perhaps the most direct single influence on English Art Nouveau was the importation of Japanese art and ideas in the latter half of the nineteenth century. Trade with Japan was made possible by the Treaty

12

of 1849 and Japan became an exhibitor in the World Exhibition of London in 1862. Before this time the words 'Japanese' and 'Chinese' were almost interchangeable to the British. The goods from China that had been imported for almost two centuries had long had their influence on the decorative arts in England. Shapes of plates and motifs for decoration are still being adapted by British potters from early Chinese porcelain. Furniture, particularly Thomas Chippendale's, and eighteenth-century interior design before the neo-classic revival, had been adapted from Chinese design. This influence became so strong that entire rooms were designed in 'the Chinese manner'. The Chinese influence showed itself again in the eclectic styles of the Victorian period of the nineteenth century. The beginnings of mass production and the machine age resulted in furniture for the growing middle class that was considered abominable by the aesthetic few.

While the more elaborate Chinese vases and dishes were the most popular among the English in the eighteenth century, the French imported the blue and white porcelain, which was simpler in design and decoration. When the Japanese finally began exporting their products to both France and England it was their blue and white porcelain that appealed most strongly to the aesthetic tastes of many artists. James McNeill Whistler collected blue and white porcelain, and he was perhaps the strongest link between British Art Nouveau and the art of Japan.

At first Whistler's interest in Japanese prints and paintings was superficial but as he came to know them better his work was the more obviously influenced by them. The Japanese prints of Hiroshige and Hokusai are strongly reflected in the arrangements of subordinate details in Whistler's large paintings; and his careful placement of his signature, the butterfly, was also borrowed from Japanese prints.

Other artistic influences were active in France in the third quarter of the nineteenth century. Although the eclectic style of decorating had become extremely popular there, too, the neo-rococo style was strong and appealed to the French taste for the more elaborate and formal. Asymmetrical design in furniture and decorative accessories was evident in this part of the century in France and the influence can be seen in later furniture of the French Art Nouveau style. The rococo style was particularly evident in the furniture made in Nancy towards the end of the century. It did not spread beyond France and Belgium, but the Gothic influence of England can be seen in some of the later work by the Nancy designers. Emile Gallé's furniture and glass from his early period are strongly rococo, but his later furniture designs have Gothic overtones.

The Gothic influence had survived in the William Morris style of decorating. Morris (1834–96) was a writer, designer, painter, decorator and socialist, who felt strongly that Victorian middle-class taste could be improved. His philosophy of grouping artists together to design and make things of simple beauty for the home became widespread. A striving for excellence in structure and design stemmed from his Arts and Crafts movement. It was important to Morris that the workshop he founded should be dedicated to changing and improving middle-class taste, but he was unsuccessful in that his hand-made artist-designed articles were too expensive for the class they were intended for. However, his philosophy of grouping talented people together for the purpose of designing wallpaper, fabric, furniture, dishes and other articles for the home in a common style, with particular emphasis on excellence of structure and design, was of far-reaching importance.

Morris, a life-long friend of Edward Burne-Jones, founded his own company and supervised the work of his associates in the decorating

*Woodblock print by Hiroshige. The importation to England and France of this type of print had a strong influence on the artists of the late nineteenth century.*

firm of Morris, Marshall, Faulkner & Company, which was founded in 1861. Carpets, wall hangings, fabrics and furniture were designed in the Gothic style. Stained-glass windows, a medium that later made Tiffany famous, were an important contribution of Morris's group. However, it was the insistence on excellence in the design and manufacture of accessories and furnishings for the home, made to blend by talented designers and craftsmen, that was the major contribution of William Morris.

In 1882 the Century Guild was founded in England by men who had been associated with William Morris and his Arts and Crafts Movement. The time was ripe for a new style and for the acceptance of original work in the decorative arts. The last quarter of the nineteenth century saw the establishment of many schools for handicrafts and the interest in the manufacture of carefully made goods for the home was as strong as the search for original design. Arthur Mackmurdo (1851–1942), Walter Crane (1845–1915) and Lewis Day (1845–1910) were active in the establishment of the Century Guild, and their designs mark the beginning of the style we now call Art Nouveau.

Walter Crane's designs for wallpaper and his book illustrations reveal the asymmetrical patterns and flat planes seen in later illustrations for books and fabric patterns made in the Art Nouveau style. Stylised flowers and foliage, asymmetrical and two-dimensional, were first used by Crane. This adaptation from nature, used in this stylised and asymmetrical manner, was an extremely important contribution to the new style. Formerly, direct copies from nature were made by designers and illustrators: the more closely an artist copied from nature, the more talent he was thought to have.

The decorative talent of Arthur H. Mackmurdo, who had also been trained with Morris's Arts and Crafts group, was a vital contribution to the Art Nouveau movement. Mackmurdo was responsible for the movement of line and undulating patterns by which we have come to identify the Art Nouveau style. He was a naturalist and trained in the Neo-Gothic tradition, but he used his training and talent to invent designs for furniture, tapestries, wallpapers and fabrics that were revolutionary for their time. His naturalistic patterns seem to float and move. Rhythm in design and the elongation of naturalistic forms can be seen in Mackmurdo's earlier work, which was to influence the designs of Charles F. Annesley Voysey (1857–1941) whose work also stressed movement and rhythm. Both these artists became more traditional as they aged, their roots remaining in the neo-Gothic movement.

*Rue Furstenburg, a lithograph by James McNeill Whistler. Note similarity of drawing of animals in lower corner of this lithograph with those in the Hiroshige print.*

An important aspect of the Art Nouveau movement in England was a renewed interest in the graphic arts. Book manufacturing had declined in quality as manufacturing processes became more modernised. The Kelmscott Press, founded by William Morris, published books that were beautiful. The illuminated page, another Morris return to Gothic influences, as well as magnificent bindings and cover designs, were to influence artists for the next thirty years.

Herbert P. Horne, another member of the Century Guild, founded 'The Hobby Horse' with Mackmurdo in 1884 in order to further interest in the new style in graphic design, and this book-periodical gave rise to many imitators. The linear designs, wavy undulating lines, and flat two-dimensional patterns of the illustrations in 'The Hobby Horse' can be seen also in 'The Dial', The Yellow Book' and 'The Evergreen'.

The epitome of this new style in drawing and illustration can be seen in the art of Aubrey Beardsley, whose work in black and white illustrations is now well known and highly appreciated for its originality

16

and style. The Japanese influence seen in the flatness of planes and rhythmic patterns of earlier innovative artists was refined by Beardsley into a style that was typically his own and highly original. This emphasis on the importance of line and movement in graphic design has had a lasting influence on graphic design and Beardsley's style has recently enjoyed a revival. The Art Nouveau style, though thought to have ended with the advent of World War I, has left its mark on much of the decorative arts and graphic design of this century.

Among the decorative periods in the past 200 years, the Art Nouveau style has been thought to have arisen suddenly and just as suddenly disappeared about thirty years later. This is not true. Now that we can view it from a distance we can see that its influences were deeply rooted in the past. The Gothic and Celtic styles in England, the rococo and to a lesser degree the baroque in France, and the very important influence of the Japanese arts and crafts all led to this original style. These influences and the talents of dedicated artists brought the Art Nouveau style to a peak, where it was taken up by mass manufacturers whose misunderstanding of the style brought about its swift decline. There are indications, however, of a lasting and important influence.

While the Art Nouveau movement began in England and had its strongest influence on the artists and designers of that country, a movement quickly sprang up in France and Belgium. As we have noted before, the French designers of furniture, glassware and ceramics differed in style from the British designers and their products were distinctively French, though the use of the undulating line, the adaptation from natural forms and the experimental work of artists and artisans were in many ways similar to the efforts of the British groups. The formation of schools and groups for the invention and execution of these new and original designs for articles to decorate the home stemmed from a combination of English influences and the tradition of the Guilds in France. The English influence in French Art Nouveau is sometimes obvious. If we recall, however, the use of naturalistic design in French decorative arts in the earlier part of the nineteenth century, when furniture was inlaid or painted with designs of realistic flowers and flower painting on plates and vases became the rage, we can see that the adaptation of these patterns by the French Art Nouveau designers to conform to the flattening of planes, the asymmetry, the undulating line and movement in design was almost inevitable.

The designs in the inlay of furniture made by Emile Gallé in Nancy are not as stylised as the English prototypes; the elongated stem and the use

*Walter Crane of the Century Guild designed this title page for The Yellow Dwarf. Crane's use of stylised plants and flowers had a strong influence on these forms when used as motifs in the decorative arts of the period. [The Christmas Tree Bookshop]*

of the ephemeral bud rather than the open flower are more typically British than French. Gallé was a naturalist and his flower designs are realistic, on his glassware as well as his furniture. However, he did use these patterns in an asymmetrical manner that seemed for the time totally original. It is interesting that, like some of the innovative English designers, Gallé's earlier work is far more experimental than his later.

The jewellery and glass designer and manufacturer, René Lalique (1860–1945), is of interest to collectors of Art Nouveau; his vases in frosty glass with opalescent raised designs and his articles of personal adornment are in the truest French Art Nouveau style. Furniture

18

designed by Hector Guimard, enamels by Emile Decoeur and pottery designed by Albert Dammouse are highly collectable and works of art of museum quality. Eugène Gaillard, Georges de Feure and Louis Majorelle also designed furniture in the French Art Nouveau manner.

A major moving spirit in the Art Nouveau world towards the end of the nineteenth century was Samuel Bing, a German, who was a publisher, art dealer and connoisseur of Japanese art in Paris. He opened a shop called Maison l'Art Nouveau that became a meeting ground for avant-garde artists and designers; and in 1895 held a Salon de l'Art Nouveau in which the works of artists such as Bonnard, Grasset, Roussel, Vuillard, Toulouse-Lautrec and others were displayed on an equal footing with the applied arts of Louis Comfort Tiffany of America, Gallé, Lalique and some of the contemporary British designers. Posters by Beardsley, Bradley and Mackintosh were also displayed, an important step in the recognition of the increasing importance of the graphic arts, which had already become collectable.

The term, Art Nouveau, stems from the name of Bing's shop and it was he who gave the movement international recognition. Before that it had gone under different names in various countries: 'Stile Liberty', 'Jugendstil', 'Sezession', were all names for the same movement. Because the new style had spread rapidly throughout the Continent and to the United States as the newest and the most modern of styles, it was hailed by contemporary critics as a complete break with the past. Styles in art, however, have never sprung into view full-grown. They have always evolved from earlier styles—at first slowly and later, as communication became more highly developed, rapidly. It is doubtful whether national styles in the decorative arts will ever be of importance again. Immediate communication with all parts of the world now make it possible for artists and designers everywhere to know what their counterparts are doing. Artistic development (or decline) has become truly international.

# 3
# How to Recognise the Art Nouveau Style

What do collectable items from the Art Nouveau period look like and how do we recognise them? There are two symbols used most frequently by designers of the Art Nouveau period, and their presence helps one to determine collectable items, though there are many other aspects of design that will help also. The first, and perhaps the symbol that was most overdone, is a woman's figure, nude, elongated and almost sexless, which was borrowed from the Pre-Raphaelite artists, who tended to use the female figure in an idealised and ethereal manner. This figure is seen on the best of Art Nouveau—and the worst. She was curled round ink-wells, pictured on vases, wrapped round clocks and held ashtrays and flowerpots aloft. She was used in drawings, paintings, posters and tapestries. Perhaps it was the commercialisation of this motif in later mass-produced items that caused the term 'Art Nouveau' to be synonymous with bad taste to the generation that grew up after the turn of the century.

Another, perhaps more important, symbol of the Art Nouveau period was the use of motifs derived but not necessarily copied from nature. Flowers, trees, insects, sea creatures and shells were used in an elongated rhythmic manner. Mackmurdo of the Century Guild was the first to use this type of decoration and he used it in the structure of furniture as well. This was perhaps the most daring type of design for the time, and in many items the decoration became more important than the structure of the article, and dictated it. Hitherto furniture had been made in more or less conventional shapes and the decoration applied to it, and the new theory of using wood in such a fluid manner was not always completely successful.

While symbols adapted from nature were used very frequently by

20

*(above) 'Ploughing'. Panel of tiles, earthenware painted in lustre. Designed by Walter Crane and made by Maw & Co about 1889. [Victoria and Albert Museum]*

*(left) Ceramic tile, probably British. [Mr and Mrs Ludy Spero]; (right) Book cover designed by Edmund Dulac (1882-1953). The face and hair of the lady are typical of the female seen as a frequent motif on art nouveau articles. [The Christmas Tree Bookshop]*

Art Nouveau artists and designers, some flowers, plants, birds and insects became most symbolic of the period. The peacock, the swan and the crane decorate many items. Whistler first used the peacock in wall decoration and Oscar Wilde used the tail feathers of the same bird in his rooms in place of flowers. Wilde, indeed, had a very strong influence on the art of the period; the sunflower was also a favourite of his and this motif is seen often, used in a drooping languid manner. Many symbols of the period drooped or curved. Emotion was applied to the decorative arts to gain an emotional effect.

Seaweed, romanticised of course, seashells, butterflies (also borrowed from Whistler) and any other natural motif that could be elongated, curved and given movement were used, most often in an asymmetrical fashion. Elongated winding stems topped with buds rather than the open blossom were a frequently used motif.

The whiplash line was an important theme used over and over again as were, indeed, all curvilinear patterns. Flat, unshaded colours in designs are also indicative of the style.

Japanese shapes and patterns influenced the Western applied arts enormously as the style developed. Whistler had been strongly influenced by Japanese woodblock prints, which were not overly popular in Japan but soon found favour with avant-garde collectors in England, the Continent and America. While symbols adapted from the Japanese arts were often used on Art Nouveau items in England, France and America, the classic shapes for vases and dishes were often directly copied, for they could hardly have been improved upon. The simple, well balanced and ideally proportioned ceramics that were being imported from Japan were ideal accessories for room decoration of the new style.

*This small bronze illustrates the use of the female figure in art nouveau, in a stylised fluid manner. Probably American. [Mr and Mrs Arthur Greenblatt]*

*American craftsmen did not, for the most part, completely grasp the concepts of British and French art nouveau designers. This silver hand-mirror has elements of both the Victorian and the art nouveau. [Jane Weber]*

By doing away with the unbearable Victorian clutter, the shapes, glazes, textures and colour of ceramic accessories for a room became extremely important to the designer. One or two simple vases in a room instead of ten or twenty elaborate ones gave more importance to the type of vase used. Liberty of London, Tiffany in New York and S. Bing in Paris all carried a large stock of Japanese imports.

Material used in room accessories became important also. New materials were tried successfully for decorative effect. In contrast to the Victorians, who used unusual material in place of the ordinary, the Art Nouveau designers tried to be honest in their approach to the materials used. Where the Victorians delighted in compressing paper or coal and using this material in place of wood, the Art Nouveau approach was to use the plainest wood without disguise. New materials were tried for decorative effects: pewter, heretofore a homely utilitarian material, was given new stature and used decoratively; stained-glass panels in furniture and windows were used in the home. More attention was given to exotic woods, but they were used in a different manner from before. Furniture was decorated with hand-painting, but with the abstract natural motifs typical of the new style. Charles Rennie Mackintosh

23

developed the idea of an all white room, the only decoration being the design, shape and decoration of the painted furniture.

Any article for the home that could be shaped into a stylised natural form was eventually designed and made. As in all decorating styles, there is good and bad in Art Nouveau. While the good designers and craftsmen were working and experimenting, most of the designs are fresh, exciting, innovative and interesting. At the turn of the century and after, mass producers adapted many of the designs in the new style to their methods of production and flooded the market with articles that they considered 'modern' and in popular demand. Art Nouveau was not a style for the masses, though many of its early proponents thought that it would be. It was too late for the hand-made carefully designed articles for the home to be made available to everyone. The Western world was still suffering from Victorian taste and often, particularly in America, the bronze clock or the nicely designed pewter ink-well were simply bought and added to the rest of the clutter. However, there were some mass-produced designs that were good and which became popular. These items were made and sold well into this century.

Many combinations of materials were used in one item. For instance, a desk might have stained glass, leather, woods and brass, and a settee might be made of wood with insets of pewter, brass or ceramic tile.

Because Art Nouveau design was more successful for the small decorative items than it was for furniture, there are a good many collectables of the period still available for the knowledgeable collector. Many of these items are artist-designed hand-made one-of-a-kind or signed

*Amateur artists were taken by the colours and motifs of art nouveau. This Limoges cache pot was exported to America undecorated where it was painted at home with peacock motifs in blue, green and gold. [Bruce Gilbert]*

*(left) 'Peacocks and Amorini': embossed leather wallpaper designed by Walter Crane (1845-1915) and printed by Jeffrey & Co, 1878. [Victoria and Albert Museum]; (above) Sconce, beaten copper embossed and chased with peacock motif. Designed and executed by Margaret and Frances MacDonald in 1896. [Victoria and Albert Museum]*

pieces, and will increase the most in value as time goes on and Art Nouveau passes from the area of collectable curiosities to the more lucrative category of the antique. Many of the signed easily recognised items are, unfortunately, already extremely expensive. Tiffany glass, which was out of favour for many years, has become almost prohibitively expensive for the average collector. Because Tiffany was the foremost American designer of Art Nouveau his vases, lamps, paperweights, etc, have been eagerly bought by dealers, collectors and museums, who realise that there is little else American to be had that is truly representative of the best of the Art Nouveau period. In a country filled with collectors it would seem that the supply of Tiffany would long since have run out, but there are still important pieces available for the affluent collector.

Just as the English are aware that Royal Doulton vases, hand-decorated, signed by the artist and one-of-a-kind are highly collectable, every other nationality tends to look for and preserve its best work. This is fortunate, for in the breakable articles there would be little left to collect if good design of any period was not recognised and preserved. This is one reason that one should collect examples of good Art Nouveau now: there are still many homes where these items are stored by descendants of the original purchasers. If we are astute enough to recognise the best of this period, these pieces, whether they end up in private or public collections, will be cared for and saved for future generations to enjoy and study.

The Art Nouveau type of design came from an intellectual-artistic theory. The groups of artists and craftsmen who were dedicated to the new style did not design their work haphazardly; they were attempting to improve the public's taste after a period of badly made, poorly designed, mass-produced home decoration. Their theories and the results did not touch the masses to any extent until much later, but they had

*(left) Pair of candlesticks, silver plate on brass. Hand-wrought in sea motif and shape. Shells and starfish raised motifs. No mark, probably American; (right) Shapes of Japanese ceramics were used frequently by British and French designers. This vase of bone china was made by Wedgwood and designed by Daisy Makeig-Jones, probably in the 1920s. [Jo-Anne Blum, Inc]*

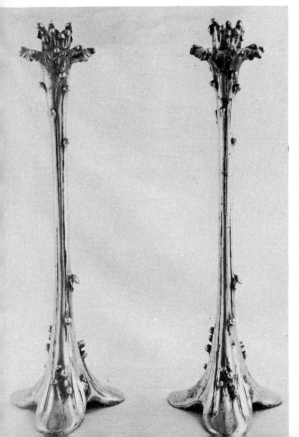

*Stylised flower forms, elongated and painted in flat tones, decorate this British humidor. [Marie Whitney Antiques]*

a lasting effect. Even the designers who started out hoping to improve the Victorians' taste could not produce goods cheaply enough for the middle and lower classes. When we balk at the present prices of Tiffany glass we should remember that it was comparatively expensive when it was new, and the fact that a Tiffany vase could have been bought for pennies in the 1930s and 1940s is only a sad commentary on our own values at that time. America remained more or less untouched by the Art Nouveau movement until the cheap mass-produced imitations flooded the market. Early Art Nouveau of the hand-made or hand-finished variety was first and foremost an English style that spread to France, Belgium, Germany, Austria and Holland. However, many of the best examples from those countries were exported to the United States, so there are items of excellent quality and design to be found almost anywhere by American collectors.

In the following chapters various types of articles made in the Art Nouveau style are discussed by category and country of origin. The collector will look for particular items that appeal to his taste and wants. The lover of books may find a volume that is representative of the graphic arts of the period or that has a binding of interesting Art Nouveau design, while those interested in ceramics may come across a plate or a vase that is hand-made, artist-decorated and unusual. We have only to train the eye to that unique style and those particular motifs that became typical of the period and to see this style, not as our parents did, with a certain disdain, but with renewed respect for the revolutionary, artistic, intellectual and fresh design that it was.

27

# 4
# Glassware

In no other material was the idea of Art Nouveau expressed in as many new ways as in glass. Vases of many different hues, decoration and shapes were made during the late nineteenth and early twentieth centuries that can never be made again. Magnificent colours and colour combinations in glass were the result of the experimentation carried on at the many glassworks in England, France, Austria and America.

A complete study of collectable art glass would be too lengthy here, so we can only point out the easily identifiable work that the collector may still find if he is fortunate and affluent. Particular stress will be placed on the two artists who stand out for their innovative and creative contributions to the art of glassmaking—Emile Gallé and Louis Comfort Tiffany.

Glass made during the period of Art Nouveau is the most sought after of all its collectables, so it has become expensive. This is not to say that the knowledgeable collector may not find an occasional bargain, but it is becoming more and more difficult to find a Tiffany or Gallé vase at a low price and one seldom hears stories about the collector who has been able to purchase these items at auction or elewhere for 'next to nothing'. Ten or fifteen years ago these items were unwanted and could be found in quantity for very little. Just as this glass was extremely popular with the generation that originally bought it when it was new, it became as unpopular with the succeeding generation.

Art Nouveau glass is symbolic of the period that it represents, most of the items designed and made, particularly by Tiffany, being completely useless. The generation that inherited this glass did not appreciate the strange forms and weird colours. It was neither 'pretty' by the standards that seem to protect breakable items through many generations, nor was it 'functional', a criterion by which items for the home were judged by the generation that grew up in the 1930s and 1940s. Therefore, it is safe to assume that a lot of important glass of the Art Nouveau period was broken and discarded before it reached its present popularity.

Although much of the art glass, because of its fragile nature, has been lost to us, there is still a large quantity that has never even come on the market. While it is likely that there is still a lot of glass stored away in attics, it is just as unlikely that this glass will eventually be sold cheaply. Prices for signed art glass have soared so rapidly in the past few years that dealers who have been able to buy look on it as an investment. Year by year the price of Tiffany and Gallé glass doubles and triples. An enormous amount of the work of both of these men was produced over the long period of time when both their companies were functioning, and their glassware seems to be the one product in which the law of 'supply and demand' has little to do with price. Art glass has become highly collectable and, therefore, highly profitable for specialist dealers, who are able, by buying every piece available to them, to control prices to a large extent.

*(left) Iridescent gold Jack-in-the-pulpit vase, signed L. C. Tiffany. [Mr and Mrs Ludy Spero]; (right) French cameo glass. Dark blue ground with pale green overlay. Signed: Gallé. [Mr and Mrs Ludy Spero]*

*(left) French cameo glass atomiser, aquamarine with black overlay decoration. [Torrington Galleries]; (right) Reverse of above showing signature: Richard.*

What are the characteristics of Art Nouveau glass? During this period of experimentation and innovation it was often given the appearance of other materials: mother-of-pearl, satin, cut velvet, lava, wood, onyx, gold, silver and ceramic-like glazes are only a few of the qualities given to it during this period. Rarely was glass left in its clear transparent condition. New methods of treating glass led to enormous variations in its appearance.

Some glassblowers were, naturally, more successful than others in what they tried to do. The colours used are, for the most part, magnificent and in many cases the combination of colour, shape and design makes many of the important pieces unique. Even a pair of vases made of hand-blown glass are never exactly alike. The best of art glass is unique in all aspects. Glassblowing is not a skill for the amateur, but requires a great amount of talent and learning. As a rebellion against the moulded glass made in huge quantities during the nineteenth century, hand-made glass revived the art of the glassblower and brought it to new heights.

In each of the decorative arts at the turn of the century there was experimentation and innovation, but nowhere did it manifest itself more strongly than in the decorative glass made by Tiffany and Gallé. In America, the name Louis Comfort Tiffany became synonymous with Art Nouveau, and had it not been for him the entire period in the decorative arts might have been ignored there. However, Tiffany glass cannot be thought of as completely 'American'. Tiffany, a talented and trained artist, who became a leading interior designer, was influenced on his trips to London by the revival of stained glass brought about by Burne-Jones and other members of the William Morris group, and he was familiar with the innovative work done by Gallé in Nancy. Tiffany, as a decorator, needed satisfactory tiles and other decorative glass for his own purposes and set about experimenting in order to produce blown glass that was decorative in itself and needed no other embellishment. Stained glass as an art form had deteriorated since the Renaissance and the glass that had been made had been overdecorated by hand. Tiffany's accomplishment was that the colour, design and density of his glass were intrinsic to the material itself, and the design of an assembled window needed no further embellishment or decoration to form the

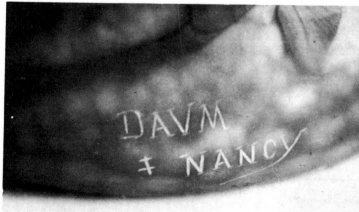

(left) French cameo glass flask. Blue ground, lavender and green design of morning glories. [Edward L. Coleman]; (below) Detail of flask showing signature: Daum, Nancy.

*Cameo glass, French, etched and hand-painted. Signed: Daum, Nancy. [Mr and Mrs Ludy Spero]*

desired picture or pattern. Tiffany's first tiles were made for lamps and lampshades and the same techniques were later applied to tiles for mosaics and stained-glass windows.

Tiffany organised a business in the applied arts that would instruct younger artists as well as produce 'art for the masses'. The Tiffany Glass Company, incorporated in 1885, produced articles of beauty for the home. For the next few years Tiffany's work in glass was mostly in the form of commissioned windows. By 1889 Tiffany had visited the shop of S. Bing in Paris and had seen the work of other artists who had chosen glass as their medium—among them Emile Gallé. The close resulting relationship of Bing and Tiffany brought about a commission for Tiffany to execute stained-glass windows to be designed by the leading artists of Bing's salon. These windows were displayed in Bing's shop.

Tiffany's workrooms, which displayed all types of articles for the home, also displayed his experimental glass. He set up his own glassworks in Corona, New York, in 1893 where experiments with glass were carried on under the supervision of Arthur Nash, an Englishman. This decorative glass was called 'Favrile'. Vases designed in many shapes, colours and sizes

32

were made according to Tiffany's philosophy that the material should be its own decoration. All the typical motifs of Art Nouveau were used: the peacock, the flower forms, Japanese shapes and motifs and the many iridescent colours that have become associated with the style. Ornament was fused into the body of the glass and opaque and matt surfaces were developed. Tiffany glass was produced until 1928 and it sold in enormous amounts.

From 1919, when Arthur Nash retired, the production of Tiffany glass was mostly orthodox, and it is the earlier experimental work that is most desired by connoisseurs. The red glass, paper-weight vases, lava vases and the fragile flower forms are highly prized today. Currently, however, anything marked or otherwise identified as having been made by the Tiffany Studios finds a willing buyer. Tiffany lamps, the same that were thrown away or stored in the attic or basement thirty years ago, have now become extremely desirable items for the collector. These lamps are important historically for their development coincided with the development of artificial light for the home in America.

The artist who exerted the strongest influence on glassmaking as an art during the Art Nouveau period was Emile Gallé of Nancy in France. Emile was the son of a glassmaker and at the age of nineteen, in 1865, he was designing glass for his father. Nine years later he had established

*Flower pot, French opalescent glass with raised motif. Signed: Lalique. [Mr and Mrs Ludy Spero]*

33

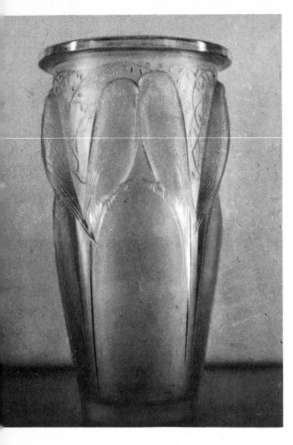

*(left) Glass vase, French. Opalescent. Signed: Lalique. [Mr and Mrs Ludy Spero]; (above) Austrian vase, signed: Loetz. [Mr and Mrs Ludy Spero]*

his own glassworks in Nancy. Energetic and artistic, Gallé studied botany and was a naturalist; and the naturalistic approach to the shape and decoration of his glass influenced all art-glass designers of the period, including Tiffany. Gallé's most frequent motifs were derived from the flowers and plants of France.

Gallé was an experimenter and he carried out systematic research in creating interesting textures and colours for his decorative glass. He used his medium in a completely free manner, unlike the makers of the classical styles of English cameo glass, and his adaptation of Thomas Webb's method of overlaying one colour of glass with another and hand-carving a design which then appeared to be sculpted and applied, led to work that was completely original.

Along with his work in creating original patterns, shapes and designs in the cameo-glass technique, Gallé experimented in opalescent and iridescent colours and also used gold leaf, which he placed between

34

layers of glass in order to create rich backgrounds for a process of enamelling he developed. Gallé was the first to use masses of mica in the body of the glass, a technique often copied by the American art-glass makers.

Because he was imaginative and energetic, Gallé tried every possible way to make his glass interesting and different from any that had been made before. His early vases required a good deal of hand-work and are by far the most collectable. When his designs started to sell well, Gallé turned out large quantities of vases and other decorative and useful items that were made by the faster process of acid etching. These vases, too, required some hand-work and Gallé chose and trained his artists and workmen with care for this job. Several of his students became well known when they started their own glassworks; among them were the Daum brothers of Nancy.

Gallé's break with the classical forms and traditional treatment of glass opened a new field for Art Nouveau designers. It is doubtful that Tiffany glass would have become as important as it did without the influence of Gallé. Coloured transparent glass, iridescent glass, layered and enamelled glass, all made in fresh shapes and forms with exciting naturalistic motifs, can be found in pieces made and signed by Gallé. Insects, tree and flower forms, as well as peacock colours and motifs were all first used by Gallé and then by Tiffany.

Gallé signed all his work, often making his signature an integral part of the design. The experimental vases, those requiring the most hand-

*Glass vase, unsigned, probably American. [Mr and Mrs Richard N. Fried]*

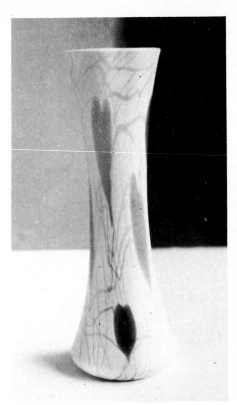

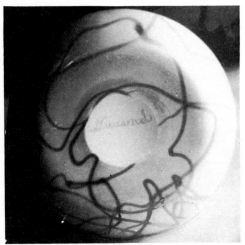

(left) Vase, white opaque glass with green design. American. [Torrington Galleries]; (below) Detail showing signature of vase.

work, were the most desirable pieces of Gallé glass when new, and are, of course, the most collectable today. The copies produced by Gallé's assistants and those that were acid-etched rather than carved by hand also bear Gallé's signature and it takes a collector who is expert on glass to distinguish between them. Most of the Gallé glass that was exported to America was of the mass-produced variety. American antique dealers are currently importing all available Gallé glass and it is possible that some early original work may be found among these imports. Even though Gallé's mass-produced glass was considered at the time it was made to have been 'copies', everything made by Gallé is worth collecting, and all his glass and that of his students is presently in demand by collectors. Gallé's glass, though signed, doesn't really need the signature to be recognised, for his unusual and strong colour combinations and his unique flower forms are typical enough.

While large quantities of art glass were made by many factories, the work of Tiffany and Gallé represents the freshest treatment of decorative glass. Many small factories and workshops sprang up at the

36

turn of the century on both continents for the design and manufacture of decorative vases and other glass objects. In Austria, iridescent glass was made in the style of Tiffany by Loetz, but it was not thought to be as successful artistically.

Kew Blas art glass, a product of the Union Glass Company of Somerville, Massachusetts, was also artistic and of high quality; it is mainly of an opalescent colour. Victor Durand, a descendant of the Baccarats of France, made art glass in Vineland, New Jersey; his glass is noted for his use of several layers of glass with threadings of coloured designs rolled between the layers. He also used the technique of laying thinly drawn threading on the outer surfaces of his vases.

The Steuben Glass Works in Corning, New York, under the directorship of Frederick Carder, produced glass that was excellent in quality, colour and design, particularly an iridescent glass called 'Aurene', which is close to Tiffany's iridescent glass in quality. It is also very similar in shape and design to Tiffany's work, so much so that it cannot be called 'innovative'. An enormous amount of 'Aurene' was produced in various colours, gold being predominant.

*(left) Vase of mica glass. Flecks of mica are embedded in the glass and applied glass threading is used to decorate outer surface; (right) Candle-vase of hand-blown glass in iridescent shades of blue, red and green. No mark.*

Due to the vast amount of experimentation and the commercial success of coloured glass during the last quarter of the nineteenth century, there are vases and other items in art glass showing every influence that the imagination of the designer could possibly conjure up. Many of the companies making decorative glass were never really touched by the Art Nouveau movement, but continued the over-decorated flowery designs of the Victorian era or the classic shapes of an even earlier period. However, all this coloured glass is in demand today by collectors.

In our concern for the innovative examples of Art Nouveau, we must be able to distinguish that glass most representative of the influences of the period. While a vase may have some innovative quality such as unusual texture, colour, interesting design, or exciting or original shape, it is the combination of all these qualities plus their genius in understanding the material that make Gallé and Tiffany the masters of this field. Placed with 100 other vases of art glass of the period a Tiffany or Gallé vase will stand out as being the most happy combination of original talent and workmanship.

Other firms experimented with glass in order to compete with Tiffany. Some of this glass represented the eclectic styles of the Victorian period, some the Japanese influence and some of it various elements of Art Nouveau; and all is highly collectable today.

Several American companies (the New England Glass Company was one) made a type of art glass called 'Peach Blow', which shaded from pale cream to a deep peach colour and was made with either a shiny or matt finish. This glass was sometimes decorated by hand with enamel or gilding or a combination of both, but generally it was left undecorated. The shapes of 'Peach Blow' vases were sometimes adapted from the Japanese vases and it is here that this glassware is most successful.

Another type of art glass, similar in appearance to 'Peach Blow', is Burmese glass, which was first produced by the Mt Washington Glass Company in 1885. Often hand-decorated, Burmese glass is shaded from pale cream to a deep salmon colour; it became very popular and was made by other companies in America and England.

The Paris designers did not neglect glassware, and Lalique designed and made unique opalescent and clear glass of high quality. August Legras also experimented with glass that was influenced by Gallé.

For the collector of art glass, there should be included here a word of warning. Now that art glass has become expensive and eagerly sought after by collectors, museums and dealers, the probability of finding 'bargains' is very slim, and it is best to deal with a reputable and know-ledgeable dealer who specialises in collectables of the period. By doing business with such a dealer, the collector protects himself from the possibility of paying a large amount of money for a copy or fake. He can avail himself of the experience and knowledge of the specialist, who will guarantee the authenticity of what he is selling. Recently the gift market has been flooded with copies of many of the art glass vases whose originals would be highly prized. These copies have been offered at so-called 'estate' auctions as being old and rare. More than once I have seen them bought for higher than retail prices.

The collector can expect the prices of Tiffany, Gallé and other art glass to be high. Nowhere is the advice of experts more valuable to the collector than in the buying of art glass. Good art glass has been coveted and collected for long enough now for it to be profitable to be copied.

Important innovative vases by Tiffany and Gallé are not likely to be picked up cheaply at street markets and antique shops. Glass is the one area of Art Nouveau collecting where one is least apt to find a bargain and most apt to be fooled.

*Small glass vase with silver overlay. American. No mark.*

# 5
# Ceramics

The return to craftsmanship in ceramics during the Art Nouveau period was as important as the developments in the arts of glassblowing and furniture design. However, ceramics of the period have, until recently, received less emphasis simply because the ceramics industry, particularly in England, was so well established that it had been thought that little innovation had taken place.

Although it is true that it was possible to turn out large numbers of any design that was thought to be saleable and marketable in this period, there were small art potteries established around this time for the manufacture of completely hand-made and hand-decorated pottery. Many first rate artists were engaged by the leading potteries to design and decorate in Art Nouveau style.

Therefore, there are two types of collectable ceramics of the Art Nouveau period: the first is the unique hand-made and hand-decorated ware of the small art potteries and the second is the pottery manufactured by the famous factories in England and on the Continent but designed and decorated by contemporary artists. There are outstanding examples of both types still available for the collector.

Ceramicists in Europe and America experimented with glazes and shapes to create new designs under the influence of the Chinese and more particularly the Japanese earthenware vases that were being collected in the Western world at the time. Influences from elsewhere were also important. William DeMorgan, an English artist who became interested in ceramics and was a friend of William Morris, adapted the lustreware designs from the seventeenth- and eighteenth-century Hispano-Moresque earthenware.

Innovation and adaptation led to exciting and interesting ceramics. This craft was given the personal attention that had been lacking for

*(above) Vases by William DeMorgan. Shapes and designs were extremely innovative and original. The lustre glaze was adapted from Hispano-Moresque earthenware. [Victoria and Albert Museum]; (left) Pottery designs by Alfred Powell. Stylised plant forms and lustre glazes were used by this designer, who worked for Wedgwood as well as other British potters. [The Studio Yearbook, 1908]*

the most part in the mass-produced pottery of the first half of the nineteenth century. Earthenware, in particular, was explored by innovators for the possibilities of new shapes and glazes.

There are two major categories of ceramics: one is the decorative, those pieces designed and executed solely for the purpose of display and decoration in the home; the second category is the useful pottery, plates and dishes of all kinds. It was mainly in the decorative ware

that Art Nouveau design manifested itself. Vases, bowls and pots of all shapes and kinds were designed and decorated in the many different motifs of Art Nouveau. The experiments with interesting and different glazes were, in most cases, highly successful.

Art Nouveau border patterns and unique shapes were designed and adapted to mass-production methods for making useful ware. The survival of many of these dishes is proof that the style was more acceptable and widespread than has been thought. For a large pottery factory to make and market sets of dishes with borders and shapes typical of one particular art style requires a large investment, and as sets of dishes do not ordinarily survive the generation for whom they were made, it is important that these patterns of Art Nouveau style are preserved as examples of the period.

### English ceramics

The end of the eighteenth century saw the beginnings of the industrial potter in England. During the nineteenth century pottery as an art declined as new ways were devised of turning out more pottery in less time, using less manpower and even less talent in the potter. While hand-painting was still used as a means of decoration on dishes, printing became the more common method of decoration. Under the influence of the Arts and Crafts movement, small art potteries opened and methods directly opposed to those of the large pottery industry in Staffordshire were started. The over-decoration of the Victorian era was abandoned by these small potters for simple and interesting shapes and glazes.

At the beginning of the twentieth century the large potteries of Staffordshire turned from the Victorian styles to the more interesting plainer pottery made by the artists. Factories such as Wedgwood, Worcester and Doultons hired art potters to experiment with new designs that could either be adapted for mass production or produced in small lots as art pottery. Wedgwood hired Alfred Powell and his wife, Louise, who designed and painted vases and plates in lustre and other 'modern' glazes. It was not until 1920, however, that a bone china body and lustre glaze typical of the Art Nouveau shapes and glazes were developed and produced at Wedgwood. This lustreware was designed by Daisy Makeig-Jones. The shapes are mostly adapted from Chinese and Japanese ceramics, but the glazes are a mottled lustre in a variety of beautiful colours. This ware, called Dragon Lustre or Fairyland Lustre, often has gold overprinting in whimsical designs of fairies, dragons, birds and butterflies. It has become highly collectable among Wedgwood collectors and Art Nouveau fanciers. Made only in decorative items, sizes range from one inch miniature wares to vases over 2ft tall. There are many sizes, colours and styles between these two extremes. Chronologically Fairy-

*(left) Salt cellar, blue and brown glaze. Marked: Royal Doulton. Initialled: L.F.; (right) Vase, pale blue glaze with darker blue glaze on raised design. Hand-painted bird motifs. Marked: Royal Doulton. [Marie Whitney Antiques]*

*(left) Pair of vases, sgraffito in-
cised design. Grey-blue glaze,
darker blue and red in design.
[Dr and Mrs David Silvert];
(above) Signature and mark on
above vases.*

land Lustre was made too late to fall within the period of Art Nouveau,
but it is certainly 'of the style' and could not belong in any other category or period. Although some mass-production methods were used in
making this ware, the nature of the glazes ensures there are no two
pieces exactly alike.

Worcester 'Sabrina' ware was developed by W. Moore Binns and
George Hancock at the turn of the century. This ware was porcelain
and had a figured glaze. Pilkington's pottery in Art Nouveau style
was made by William and Joseph Burton, who experimented with lustre
glazes. Many of these wares were signed by the artists who decorated
them. Gordon Forsyth and E. C. Cundall were two artists who worked
on Pilkington's art ware.

William Moorcroft of Burslem made art pottery in quantity with
heavy glazes and sgraffito decoration. Many of these highly successful
pieces are signed and numbered, and some of the vases are dated.
Moorcroft pottery is a fine example of matching shape and decoration
to one another. Often in this kind of pottery the design is raised in
outline and the glaze is adapted to the design. Moorcroft pottery is
at present highly collectable.

The industrial pottery production is better known than that of the many small art potteries and family concerns, which produced pottery in much smaller quantity. Ceramics, by its very nature, involves the talents of chemists as well as artists and the larger potteries were set up for the kind of experimentation that was necessary to produce the new lustre glazes and innovative shapes. On the whole, the pottery production in Art Nouveau styles lasted longer into the twentieth century than most of the other decorative arts, and we find English art pottery in the style of Art Nouveau until around 1930.

## French ceramics
French ceramics were designed in Art Nouveau style by artists who were already involved with other media. Ernest Chaplet and Auguste Deleherche designed decorative ware adapted from the Japanese vases that S. Bing displayed in his shop in Paris. As in England, earthenware was more readily used for experimentation than porcelain. Paul Gauguin,

*(left) Dragon lustre vase designed for Wedgwood by Daisy Makeig-Jones. Bone china, blue lustre glaze with gold printed design. Marked: Wedgwood Bone China, Made in England; (right) Fairyland lustre plate designed by Daisy Makeig-Jones. Marked: Wedgwood Bone China, Made in England. [Mr and Mrs Ludy Spero]*

*(left) Tableware, pearlware body. Blue, red and green printed pattern. Marked: Saxon, Wedgwood, Etruria, England, William H. Plummer Co. New York; (right) Coffee pot, part of set made in England for American market. Marked: Rich and Fisher, New York, copyright Novem Artem, Made in England. [Jane Weber]*

the artist, experimented with ceramics and made vases that verged on the abstract, but it is extremely unlikely that any collector today would come across a Gauguin vase.

Factories in France adopted some of the designs of the experimental artists in their production of porcelain and pottery. Occasionally one finds products of the various factories at Limoges in patterns and shapes that can be from no period other than that of the turn of the century.

The Art Nouveau movement in ceramics was widespread in France. Emile Gallé of Nancy, though noted mainly for his work in glass, also designed and manufactured art pottery. While Gallé pottery is not as successful artistically as his glass, his ceramics are quite collectable. As in his other work, all pieces were signed and are, therefore, easily identifiable. Most of the existing pieces of Gallé pottery have heavy glazes and the shapes are not specially graceful.

### Dutch ceramics

Perhaps the most innovative and original of all Art Nouveau ceramics was the semi-porcelain decorative ware made by Rozenberg of the Hague, a firm operating from 1894 to 1916. J. Jurriaan Kok and J. Schelling designed vases and tea-sets for Rozenberg from an

46

extremely thin ceramic body that was blown rather than modelled. The decoration for these vases was adapted from Javanese batik designs rather than the Japanese adaptations that were being used in England and France.

Kok designed the forms and Schelling the decoration, but the integration of design and form of these pieces to the unique material used as a body makes them the gems of all Art Nouveau ceramics. The semi-vitreous body is extremely fragile and almost paper thin, and the decoration is almost as fragile in appearance as the body. The bottle vases made with handles that pull away from the body are quite rare because of the fragile nature of the material used, but each is as much a work of art in ceramics as the finest Tiffany vase is in glass.

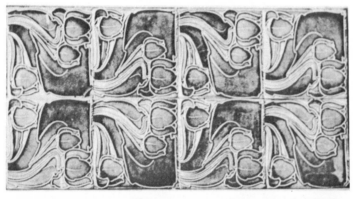

*Tile designs in ceramics became important for interior decoration. The ceramics industry in England sponsored schools to train young designers. These two designs were made by students of the Burslem Art School in 1906. [The Studio, Volume 37, 1906]*

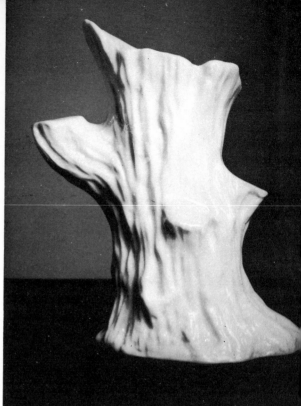

*(above) Basalt flower holder in organic form. Marked: Wedgwood, England; (right) Irish Belleek vase in natural form of tree trunk. Creamy glaze on exterior, saffron iridescent yellow glaze inside.*

T. A. C. Colenbrander also designed ceramics for Rozenberg. He adapted his designs from batik patterns and worked in a heavier clay than did Schelling and Kok. His use of background in the patterns of decoration was innovative in that the white glaze of the pottery itself was as important to the designs as the applied decoration. Strong colours and abstract design in ceramics decoration were Colenbrander's contributions.

### Hungarian ceramics
Vilmos Zsolnay, together with a chemist, discovered a red-glazed ceramic body that took iridescent over-glazes well. The Zsolnay pottery in Pecs, Hungary, made and exported decorative ceramics in Art Nouveau style for several years at the turn of the century. Many of the existing pieces of Zsolnay are hand-made serpent shapes of coiled clay.

### German ceramics
Henry Van de Velde designed patterns for the decoration of useful ware, and like his designs for other items, Van de Velde's pottery

decoration was abstract and ahead of its time. He liked to adapt the new designs to articles of everyday use rather than to the decorative items produced by other potters and decorators.

Just as in England and France, the national porcelain and pottery factories re-evaluated their styles during this period and small ateliers produced art pottery. Meissen was one of the larger factories to produce artist-designed pottery and porcelain in the new style. Art Nouveau motifs, the dragonfly, flowers, sea animals and plants were motifs used frequently and flower forms were used for vase shapes.

## American ceramics

Perhaps the most outstanding of all American Art Nouveau pottery is that made by the Rookwood Pottery in Cincinatti, Ohio. This firm was founded by a woman, Mrs Marion Longworth Storer, a Cincinatti socialite, who became interested in ceramics through her association with the Pottery Club in that city—founded originally for teaching china painting to ladies.

The Rookwood Pottery, under Mrs Storer's leadership, became a

*(left) Earthenware vase. Signed: Emile Gallé. [Victoria and Albert Museum]; (right) Earthenware vase, glazed in red and brown. Maker unknown. Marked: France. [Jane Weber]*

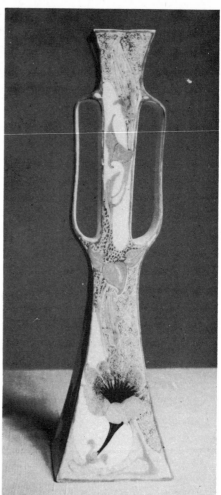

(top) Porcelain candy dish, iridescent mother-of-pearl glaze inside, abstract hand-painted design, gold, green and blue. Marked: B & Co., Limoges, France, A. H. G.; (above) Candy dish, porcelain, hand-painted in dark blue and gold. Marked: Limoges, France. [Jane Weber]; (top right) Bottle vase, porcelain, Dutch. Hand-painted in orange and green; (right) Mark on bottom of above vase showing company that made it and the marks of the artists who designed and painted it (Rozenberg, Kok, Schelling).

*(left) Bottle vase, red earthenware body, iridescent blue-green glaze over fish-scale design: (above) Detail showing mark on above vase made in Pecs, Hungary.*

highly successful business, its major product being decorative vases. Hand-work and hand-decorating led to the production of individual pieces of pottery strongly influenced by the oriental shapes and glazes and the naturalism then being used by contemporary artists. A Japanese, Kataro Shirayamadani, was one of Mrs Storer's chief decorators. All pieces were marked with either **Rookwood Pottery, Ohio** (from 1880–2), **Rookwood** (impressed in the clay, 1882–6) and thereafter, **RP** and a sunburst with additional rays added for each year after 1886. The glazes typical of Rookwood pottery are browns, reds and yellows heavily and richly applied. 'Tiger's Eye' is a glaze containing gold flecks and anything made by Rookwood with this glaze is very desirable to collectors of American Art Nouveau.

Other potteries that were developed after the Rookwood firm in America and which made decorative ware similar to Rookwood were the Weller Pottery in Zanesville, Ohio, and the Hampshire Pottery in Keene, New Hampshire. The work of these two firms is often confused with that of Rookwood, but usually the quality of glaze and shape of the ceramics are not as successful artistically.

Louis Comfort Tiffany made ceramics in a unique style: the stylised

51

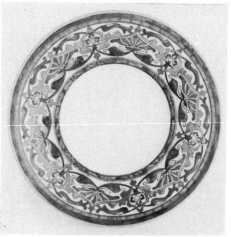

*A great deal of 'whiteware' or undecorated porcelain was exported to America from France at the beginning of this century. It was then decorated by amateurs at home. These two plates are particularly successful examples of the work that became a hobby for ladies. Both plates are marked: Limoges and signed by the artist, Louise C. Hanford.*

plants and flower forms of the period were used to decorate many of his wares and the designs were often used in relief. Usually the relief work was the only decoration on these mainly unglazed vases. Bronze glazes were sometimes used by Tiffany as well as a matt glaze that had a crystalline effect. Bases for lamps were made of pottery at the Tiffany Studios, but rather late, and it is doubtful whether Tiffany designed any of these lamp bases himself.

After the influence of the Arts and Crafts movement became strong in America individuals and groups established small art potteries whose products can sometimes be found by the collector. Many of these pieces are unmarked and it depends on the collector's judgement and knowledge as to what combinations of qualities lead to successful pottery design and execution whether he is going to invest in unmarked work. Perhaps the most important criterion for successful hand-made pottery is the relationship of the glaze and other decoration to the shape and body of the item. The collector must bear in mind the influences of the period, and if a vase shows strong Japanese influence or if organic flowing lines of the art style are carried out successfully the item is probably a wise investment.

52

*(above left) Vase, earthenware. American. Dark brown glaze, yellow hand-painted leaf motif. Marked: Owens; (above right) Jug, hard paste. American. Ears of corn hand-painted. Manufactured by Ott & Brewer, Trenton, New Jersey. Marked: Belleek. Artist H. W. Sparadin, 1903. Made by the Ceramic Art Co, Trenton, NJ, forerunner of Lenox; (below) Earthenware vase, American. Brown glaze with yellow flower motif. Silver overlay. No mark.*

53

# 6
# Furniture

Art Nouveau design was generally more successful in smaller accessories for the home than it was in the manufacture of furniture. Not a lot of furniture was made considering that the movement became so widespread. Even after the designers and manufacturers took up the style for the mass market, no large quantities of furniture were produced. Here and there in the mass-produced furniture of the period, particularly in America where there was no one outstanding designer of Art Nouveau furniture, can be seen the influence in carved or painted motif. An oak desk or chair may carry this type of decoration, but the basic lines of the furniture are the same that were used earlier.

There were some designers working mainly in England, Scotland and France whose work was highly successful artistically but whose designs called for hand-carving and decorating, so that these designs were difficult or impossible to adapt for the mass market. The innovative Art Nouveau furniture that survives today was made mostly by hand and many of the pieces are one-of-a-kind. Most of the designs are fresh and original, with influences of the Gothic in England and the rococo in France. Most of the hand-made furniture of the period is either signed or can be attributed to one particular designer or architect, or to the groups of craftsmen who worked together to make it, which is an enormous advantage to curators, dealers and collectors.

Experimentation was important to the designers of furniture in the new style, though the designs fall into only two major categories: those pieces that depend upon flat two-dimensional decoration such as inlay, painted design, applied metal or glass, or the use of fabric in the design; and the other, more typically French, method of using the wood itself as a material for sculpted form. The first type of design was structurally more successful simply because wood grain does not adapt itself easily to the fluidity demanded by some of the French designers. The first

*Armchair, oak inlaid with ebony, with panels of rush in the seat and back. Designed by E. G. Punnett and made by Wm Birch, Ltd, High Wycombe, in 1901. [Victoria and Albert Museum]*

method of design and decoration was used by the British and more closely reflects the strong influence of the Morris Arts and Crafts movement.

## British furniture

British designers experimented with the use of unusual woods, though oak and ash were used most frequently. Highly polished dark woods were mostly ignored. Around 1900 certain British manufacturers adapted the Art Nouveau designs to production for the mass market and there are some pieces of furniture seen on the market today that are successful in design and quite decorative. China cabinets in particular adapted to the style commercially because they could be made in fairly simple style and depended upon coloured glass panels in the doors for decoration. The designs used in these glass panels are often the elongated flower, stem and bud patterns in Art Nouveau style.

Although all part of the same movement with essentially the same philosophy of total integration of room furnishings expressed in a totally new way, the furniture of England, France, Germany and Scotland is easily identifiable nationally. The earliest influences in English Art Nouveau style in furniture as well as the rest of the decorative arts grew out of Morris's Arts and Crafts neo-Gothic style.

The aim of the Century Guild (1882) was to restore the decorative arts to the hands of the artist rather than the tradesman, and members of the Guild were involved in architecture, pottery, wood-carving, metalwork and all the decorative arts as well as the fine arts. A. H. Mackmurdo was responsible for many of the designs of objects made by the members, and his work is the earliest manifestation of a break with the past and the innovative use of the fluid elongated line that influenced the entire period of Art Nouveau design.

One of the foremost British designers of furniture was C. R. Ashbee, who was also a writer. Ashbee formed the Guild of Handicraft in 1888 for the purpose of designing and making decorative objects in wood and metal. Furniture made by such groups is usually very scarce. A catalogue of an exhibit of 'Victorian and Edwardian Decorative Arts'

*(left) Chair, oak, designed by C. F. A. Voysey. [Studio Yearbook of Decorative Art, 1908]; (right) Table, oak, designed by C. F. A. Voysey. [Studio Yearbook of Decorative Art, 1908]*

held at the Victoria and Albert Museum in 1952 describes one of Ashbee's designs as 'Cabinet (Height 4ft 7in, Width 3ft 6in, Depth 1ft 10in) walnut, the interior of silver-grey with red morocco leather tooled in gold. Externally, tooled leather, with polished iron fittings. Made by J. W. Payment and others, the Guild of Handicraft (leather by Stacia Power): about 1903'. The description of this piece from a private collection demonstrates the method of working together that was the purpose of the various guilds. Eventual owners benefited from the talents of not one but many good artists and craftsmen.

Mackay Hugh Baillie Scott was an architect and designer who began working in private architectural practice at the turn of the century. His designs for furniture were made up by several different manufacturers of fine furniture, notably Broadwood and J. P. White. He was more important as an innovative architect, but Baillie Scott demonstrated in his furniture designs the use of many different materials such as leather, pewter, ivory, copper and brass as decoration. The furniture he designed was made to be used in houses of his design, and he also designed a quantity of built-in furniture.

Charles F. A. Voysey was another British architect who designed furniture. He was influenced by Mackmurdo and also designed textiles. His furniture, made of oak, showed the strong influence of Morris's Arts and Crafts group. Voysey often used brass hinges and fittings on his case furniture, the metal most often having cut-out two-dimensional designs as decoration. His chairs had straight backs and rush seats. Voysey's furniture was conservative in style, well made, and a complete departure (regardless of the evidence of the Morris influence) from any of the furniture styles that had come before. Various makers executed Voysey's designs for him: C. F. Nielson, W. H. Tingey, J. Coote, William Hall and Storey & Co were some of them.

Other British designers, who formed the firm of 'Kenton & Co' in 1890 in Bloomsbury, were Ernest Gimson, Mervyn McCartney, W. R. Lethaby and R. Blomfield. This firm lasted only two years, but the idea on which it was formed—to design and make furniture in the 'New Style' with each designer supervising the work of the hired cabinet-makers who executed the designs—was in the true Arts and Crafts tradition. After 'Kenton & Co' closed, Gimson, with Sidney and Ernest Barnsley, set up a workshop that was somewhat more successful commercially. These designers experimented with the use of unusual and interesting materials and their furniture has inlays of ivory, ebony, tooled leather and mother-of-pearl.

By the turn of the century, furniture manufacturers in England, looking for new designs, took up the ideas of the innovators and adapted them for mass production. One of these companies whose work was more successful than others was Heal & Co, whose furniture used materials and designs already tried by the craftsmen of the Guilds. Oak inlaid with ebony, pewter, ivory and mother-of-pearl was used for much of this production. Even though methods of mass production were used in the manufacture of Heal's furniture, the finishing had to be done by hand, and the best available craftsmen were employed on this work.

A lecture on Arts and Crafts given at the Glasgow School of Art in 1893 by its principal, Francis H. Newberry, inspired students of design at the school to do work in the new style. The leader of this group, Charles Rennie Mackintosh, was its outstanding designer. He designed

*(above) English desk, walnut with various woods inlaid. Stained glass back, tooled leather top; (right) Tall case clock, English. Hand-carved art nouveau decoration. [Marie Whitney Antiques]*

58

furniture that is almost completely original and yet belongs to the category of Art Nouveau. His designs were sculptural in quality and he employed the use of enamelled paint as a finish; he also used patterns of inlaid materials, including metals and semi-precious stones. Mackintosh exhibited in Glasgow, Vienna, Liège, Budapest, Dresden, Munich and Venice and his work had a strong influence on designers of furniture everywhere.

Mackintosh's wife, Margaret Macdonald, was also educated at the Glasgow School of Art and was strongly influential in her husband's work. She often decorated his furniture and exhibited her gesso panels, stained glass and metalwork along with it.

For the collector, good examples of English Art Nouveau furniture will be difficult to find, chiefly because the British have understood their importance in the movement and have taken care that the available good pieces by recognised innovators of the period and style are purchased for museums and kept in the country. Although most of these pieces do not yet have antique value, they are extremely important artistically and historically. Because the Art Nouveau movement stemmed from British artists and craftsmen and because there was not a lot of furniture made to begin with, it is rare that a piece comes up for sale in the auction rooms. When it does, however, it is worth almost any price one is forced to pay. It represents the last hand-crafted, original design in furniture that the world is apt to see. Many of these pieces are one-of-a-kind and most of the work in them is entirely original. So far, no one has attempted to reproduce these designs, though that likelihood is not far off.

**French furniture**
While it is difficult to discuss the Art Nouveau design of any one nation without referring to what was being done elsewhere, in furniture there were distinctive styles that were typically French and others that were typically English or German. In order to distinguish the qualities that belonged to artists working in the various areas it is therefore necessary to consider the designers geographically, keeping in mind that all were exposed to the work of each other at the exhibitions that were popular all over Europe at the time.

The two cities in France that produced the few outstanding designers of French furniture in Art Nouveau style were Paris and Nancy. The showcase for all French designers working in the new style was Bing's shop in Paris. As with Emile Gallé, the designers often worked in more

Small table, French. Designed and made by Emile Gallé. Hand-carved and inlaid with various woods. Three views showing front, top detail and signature.

than one medium, so that of necessity they must be discussed in more than one chapter.

Emile Gallé's furniture showed the great skill in design and craftsmanship that was evident in his glass. Gallé used floral forms in a fresh new fashion, first, in the structure of his early furniture where the entire piece shows an organic feeling, and, later, in the decoration only, as in the table shown on p60. In this small table the inlay is used in a manner that is typical of both the period and the style, illustrating the asymmetrical aspects of design. The design of the legs and overall design of the table are rather conventional, however, differing from the early work done by Gallé. For this reason, Gallé's later tables are not out of place with conventional furniture and have become popular for the eclectic collector and decorator today. The table top illustrates the use of various kinds of wood for contrast and colour tones and the hand-carving in the design creates a three-dimensional effect.

While many plant and flower forms were used by Gallé in the marquetry of his furniture, the iris seems to be the most prevalent. The tables were all signed, usually in inlay as part of the decoration. Smaller signatures were used on the later, more conservative, tables. Some of the earlier tables of the more fluid designs are two-tiered with inlay on both trays.

It is not difficult to recognise Gallé furniture, nor is it too difficult at present to find a small Gallé table in the antiques markets on both continents, for his tables are not yet priced out of reach of the average collector. At present the market price of a small Gallé table is no higher than the cost of a good, new, mass-produced end table. If any Art Nouveau furniture is going to rise in value, however, Gallé's will certainly be among it. Most of Gallé's pieces are small and usable with other styles of furniture in today's smaller homes and apartments, and there is never a question as to the maker or quality of design. For the collector who is searching for beauty and good investment, there is nothing of the period more promising than Gallé furniture. A table can often be bought for less than one of Gallé's vases, because of the demand by collectors for all signed art glass and the fact that there are many more glass than furniture collectors. Also many dealers as well as collectors are not aware that Gallé made furniture as well as glassware.

Louis Majorelle was another important designer of Art Nouveau furniture, and lived and worked in Nancy. Majorelle handled wood in the manner of a sculptor, modelling rather than building; his work has

*(left) Corner cupboard from Castel Henrietta, Sèvres, designed by Hector Guimard in 1902; (above) Detail of Guimard cupboard showing excellent use of grain of wood in design. [John Jesse]*

a more daring, fluid appearance than Gallé's and he is always innovative. His metal forms were botanical derivations as were Gallé's, and both men were strongly influenced by Japanese designs; yet there is something about their designs that is obviously French. Majorelle carried Gallé's designs further than Gallé, himself, was willing to do, but both men designed furniture that is aesthetically successful in every way.

Of the artists designing in Paris, de Feure, Gaillard, Selmersheim, Plumet and Collona were the major figures, their complete rooms being displayed in Bing's Gallery. Their work was lyrical and innovative, but next to the outstanding Paris architect and designer, Hector Guimard, secondary in importance. Guimard's furniture showed a complete break with the traditional and he became the first of the designers of free-form furniture, beautiful, carefully constructed and functional. Although fluid in line, the wood grains and the design seem to be in perfect harmony, great attention having been paid to the detail in carving.

Examples of Guimard's and Majorelle's furniture come up for sale from time to time, usually at the leading auction houses or at specialist dealers in Art Nouveau. Good furniture, before it is officially antique, is always recognised and collected by connoisseurs; and, fortunately, the best pieces are seldom discarded even when they go out of style. The prices for the major pieces of furniture, particularly in French Art Nouveau style, are currently quite high; but since there was so little made, the prices will go even higher, for there is not even enough available to supply the major museums who have just begun to collect furniture of this period in any quantity. This is the time for the wise and affluent collector to invest in what is certain to be the next desirable important form of antique.

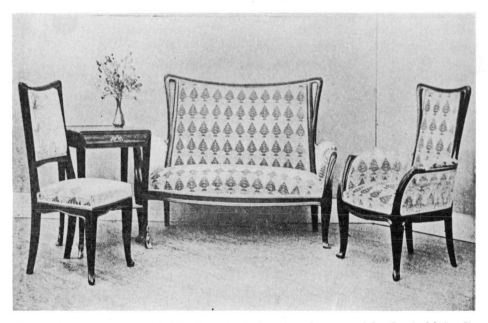

*Loveseat, two chairs and table, French, designed and executed by Louis Majorelle.* [The Studio Yearbook of Decorative Art, *1908*]

63

*Desk and chair, French, designed and executed by Louis Majorelle.* [The Studio Yearbook of Decorative Art, *1908*]

The designers of Belgium provided a link between the flat two-dimensional designs of England and the fluid rococo patterns of the French. Victor Horta, the Belgian architect, brought the decorative arts of the period to a new height by designing all the ornaments for his rooms in such a fashion that he subordinated the materials used to the fluidity of his designs. Gustave Serrurier-Bovy combined French and English influences but his work emphasised the flat quality of the British designers and was less plastic and fluid than Horta's.

Henry Van de Velde, mentioned earlier, turned from the fine arts to the decorative arts under the influence of Morris and Ruskin. His work embraced all facets of the decorative arts including designs for women's clothing and jewellery and his furniture was an expression of his philosophy of doing away with organic and natural forms and expressing the same idea in the abstract. Ornament was not used on Van de Velde's furniture and the lines became the important detail. Van de Velde's ultimate influence on later abstract and functional designs is important.

# 7
# Jewellery

One area of Art Nouveau collecting that is now enyoying a revival is that of jewellery. The jewellery of this period was, for a long time, unwanted. A vase or a pair of candlesticks might blend with articles of other styles in the home, or might have been bought because their design appealed to the buyer, but jewellery is seldom bought for any reason than it is in fashion. Art Nouveau jewellery was out of fashion for a long time. Naturally, jewellery made of valuable materials was not thrown out and gold, silver and precious stones are not often treated carelessly. Because Art Nouveau jewellery is, perhaps more than any other collectable of the period, so representative of its period, women would not wear it once the fashion was over.

The general characteristics of the jewellery made during the Art Nouveau period must be discussed in relation to women's fashion of the time and to their way of life during the years directly before and after the turn of the century. With the close of the Victorian period came the emancipation of women and the revolt of the younger generation. Women of good families, for the first time in history, began to value their own identities and went out to pursue education and careers of their own. Fashion became more emancipated, too. The elaborate dress and overabundant use of heavily designed jewellery that had been fashionable for the Victorian lady was not pleasing nor practical for the newly emancipated woman; she wanted new styles in jewellery and clothing to match her new way of life. Less and less jewellery was worn in the daytime as the nineteenth century drew to a close. The heavy chains and dog collars went out of fashion and jewellery was designed on a lighter scale than before.

The designers began to replace precious stones with semi-precious. Hitherto, the size of a brooch and the precious stones it contained had constituted the importance of a piece of jewellery, but now the design and the adaptation of that design to the materials came to be more important. The Arts and Crafts movement influenced jewellery design as strongly as it did the decoration for the home.

In general, Art Nouveau jewellery differed from Victorian in combining less expensive materials with first-class design, and in using Art Nouveau motifs such as the peacock, tendril shapes, flower forms, the human face (often that of Sarah Bernhardt), and insect motifs realistically or fancifully. Often the cabuchón shapes in semi-precious stones dictated the asymmetrical design of a brooch or ring. Coloured enamel was often used as a decoration for silver and gold work.

Because of the new informality, sporting jewellery became popular and brooches of gold and precious or semi-precious stones were designed in the shapes of horseshoes, foxes, hounds and horns. Bracelets were made with thin wires rather than heavy links. Cross-over motifs were used on bracelets and rings, thereby interpreting the asymmetrical spirit of Art Nouveau. For the first time, important jewellery was designed by artists who worked in other media and it is these pieces that are the most collectable. Often they are not made of precious stones and gold, and it is the designs themselves that give these unusual pieces of jewellery their importance. It is not unusual

*Enamelled gold pendant, English. Designed and executed by Phoebe Traquair.* [The Studio, *1906*]

*Advertisement for hand-made jewellery from* The Studio, *Vol 37, 1906, illustrates the use by British designers of natural shaped semi-precious stones and hand-wrought metal.*

to see diamonds set in silver, or semi-precious stones set in gold. A silver brooch designed by C. R. Ashbee of the Arts and Crafts group is as important as a piece of jewellery designed by a lesser artist in gold set with diamonds. It is the design that matters.

While all the usual items of jewellery were made in the Art Nouveau style, it is in the larger pieces that the major artists of the period best expressed the new intellectual aproach to design. Brooches and large pendants head the list of important pieces of Art Nouveau jewellery. Another item, which depended upon the contemporary women's style

*Small silver brooch, British, enamelled in red and green. Hallmarked for 1906.*

of wearing ribbon and fabric belts on their Edwardian dresses was the belt buckle, made in two parts connecting in the centre. Many of these buckles were major pieces of jewellery, but because they, above all other items made, depended on the fashion, they have only so far been collected as oddities and for their intrinsic beauty and value. Since fashion historically repeats itself, it is not unlikely that those women who own these magnificent buckles will one day wear them again.

Perhaps the most important of the early Art Nouveau style jewellery of England was designed by Charles Robert Ashbee, who was chief designer for the Guild of Handicraft, which he also founded. Ashbee's designs for personal ornament, as well as his designs for furniture and other objects for the home, were executed by craftsmen hired by the Guild. He used gold and silver and precious and semi-precious stones. Existing examples of brooches and pendants show that he often used the peacock motif. Cabuchón stones and baroque pearls were favourites with him and many of his pieces use several kinds of metal together with enamelling and stones. Tendrils and leaves form many of his pins and brooches. Some of his pieces were enormous by present-day standards: one peacock-shaped brooch, for instance, is $4\frac{5}{8}$in high by

$2\frac{3}{8}$in wide, made in silver, with gold and silver applied ornament, and set with mother-of-pearl, diamonds and semi-precious stones. The peacock's eye was a ruby.

While some of Ashbee's designs might be rather ostentatious and elaborate for modern taste, he also designed some small circular and crescent-shaped brooches that would be very wearable today. One round silver brooch of leaves and tendrils set with a round amethyst is very acceptable today, and a crescent of graduated moonstones is the kind of jewellery that is never out of favour.

It is possible that the important large pieces of jewellery designed by Ashbee were made for exhibition purposes or to special order. In any case, Ashbee's designs strongly encouraged other designers of the period to make what was then considered 'modern' jewellery. Other important designers and innovators of English Art Nouveau jewellery were Arthur Gaskin and his wife, G. E. Sedding, Phoebe Traquair, Nelson and Edith Dawson, Henry Wilson, Richard Rathbone, Charles de Sousy

*Russian bracelet, gold with topaz, having carved ivory head. Possibly Fabergé. [John Walters]*

Ricketts, John Paul Cooper, Harold Stabler, Omar Ramsden and Houghton Maurice Bonner. These designers influenced the commercial jewellers, many of whom sent their work to exhibitions, and by 1900 many pieces of minor jewellery for the everyday trade were being made in the Art Nouveau style in England.

## French jewellery

France has always understood women and fashion better than any other nation and has continually set the styles in clothing and adornment for the rest of the western world. In jewellery design perhaps more than in any other area, French Art Nouveau expressed itself in its purest and most original style. The forms and motifs that were adapted for other forms of Art Nouveau by the French were also used in jewellery design. Insects, plants with undulating stems and leaves, birds, and women's faces and figures were the motifs often used. The materials were similar to those used by the English designers. Baroque pearls and cabuchón stones appeared frequently, as did high-quality enamelwork

The Japanese influence, particularly a reverence for asymmetry, showed itself strongly in French jewellery designs. As with English Art Nouveau jewellery, the design of the whole was of primary importance, and we see intricate designs in combs, brooches, buckles and pendants.

The most important name in French Art Nouveau jewellery design is that of René Lalique. Lalique was the first of the French designers to emphasise design and artistic interest, rather than the value of the material used. The market was good, for jewellery was still being worn in abundance by the French woman of fashion at the turn of the century: decorative combs for the hair, enormous hatpins, necklaces, brooches and buckles.

As valuable stones became less important than design and the use of interesting materials, the baroque pearl, opals and other semi-precious stones came to be used in the large baroque-like pieces. Dragonflies, lizards, snakes, swans and other prototypes from nature, embellished and always created in movement, adorned the bosoms of fashionable ladies.

At the turn of the century elegant jewellery for men was also designed. Homosexuals became socially acceptable in France, and as they required the latest in fashion, jewellery was designed for them in the new style.

*Cross-over design was used often for rings and bracelets. This small ring is gold set with turquoise and seed pearls.*

Besides Lalique, other French designers of Art Nouveau jewellery were Paul Albert Beaudoin, Charles Fouquet and Carl Fabergé, and their designs were adapted by other craftsmen and artists working at the same time. In the fashion of the period, Mucha, the poster artist, who worked almost exclusively for Sarah Bernhardt, also designed jewellery for the actress, much of it portraying her own face and figure. Hector Guimard, better known for his furniture designs, made jewellery in abstract rather than naturalistic motifs.

Much of the Art Nouveau jewellery that remains owes its survival to the fact that it was not made from precious stones. Usually, when diamonds or other stones of great value are used in pieces of jewellery of a particular style, those pieces are broken up and the stones reset as the style changes. Since many of the important pieces of Art Nouveau jewellery depend more on the design than the value of the stones, a lot of it was tucked away and forgotten, only to be taken out in the past few years as the Art Nouveau style has been revived. These pieces are often priced according to the importance of the designer

*Silver ring, hand-wrought, mother-of-pearl stone. Baroque shells were used often in inexpensive American jewellery. [Mrs Hayden Alexander]*

and maker, when they can be identified, or according to the materials they were made of; so it is still possible to find inexpensive pieces of Art Nouveau jewellery of good design. Naturally, the most desirable pieces are those that are wearable by today's standards. Enormous dragonfly corsages and peacock brooches, no matter how beautiful the workmanship, materials and design, do not appeal to the modern collector as jewellery to be worn, but as collector's items that can be displayed. For the purposes of art history these large and elaborate pieces should be carefully preserved, for the artistry and workmanship that went into their manufacture has all but disappeared today.

Once the important designers had set the style, many of the commercial jewellers designed and made pins, brooches, necklaces, rings and bracelets smaller in scale but obviously of the period. Silver pins, beautifully enamelled, can still be bought cheaply in the street markets in London and Paris, their price ordinarily depending on the weight of the silver. Rings in Art Nouveau style are not as readily available. Many of the rings currently found have been made from buttons that were issued in sets.

As long as Art Nouveau jewellery is not considered to be 'antique' it will not be overpriced. Victorian jewellery has increased in value considerably in the past ten years, since it has become fashionable again; but for the collector who is willing to search among the older pieces of jewellery for the slightly newer but more unusual designs of Art Nouveau, there are many exciting bargains still available.

# 8
# Metalwork

The use of metals for decorative objects made in Art Nouveau style for the home was revolutionary. Experiments were made with metals that had not been used decoratively before. Copper, pewter and wrought-iron often replaced precious materials such as silver and gold, though these materials were not overlooked. The best of the metal objects made in Art Nouveau style were artist-designed and made partly or entirely by hand, though many successful objects were also mass-produced.

Just about anything that had previously been made to decorate the home in metal was made again in Art Nouveau style: boxes, candlesticks, flatware, vases, plates, goblets, coffee- and tea-sets. Useful as well as decorative objects were designed and made, often from the less precious metals such as copper, brass or pewter. Frequently several different metals were used most successfully on the same object. The methods of decoration comprised chasing, embossing, applied metal on metal, and inlay of metal or sometimes semi-precious stones. For many pieces the shape was all and extraneous decoration was avoided, and shapes followed Art Nouveau principles, being organic, fluid and often asymmetrical. Cloisonné and enamelwork were often used as decoration.

Metalwork in Art Nouveau style is perhaps the most fertile area in which the collector can search. Metal, by its very nature, is a lasting material. It does not break and, therefore, there is still a large supply available; when Art Nouveau went out of fashion, no one threw away a silver box or picture frame. Wrought-iron candlesticks might be stored in the attic or basement, but they were less likely to have been thrown out or sold to the junkman than the chipped plate or the broken chair.

*Jewel box, wood mounted with beaten brass, set with opalescent glass. Signed: Ch. Rennie Mackintosh. Made about 1897 for Jessie Keppie to whom he was then engaged. [Victoria and Albert Museum]*

In the more precious metals such as silver or bronze the owner who might not have appreciated the design did appreciate the intrinsic value of the metal. As many of the metal Art Nouveau objects are not signed, the value of the well designed pieces is sometimes not recognised by owners and the collector can sometimes find museum-quality collectables at comparatively low prices. The collector, however, must be able to recognise those qualities of design typical of Art Nouveau, by studying an object to tell whether any hand-work was used in its making, and, hopefully, to recognise the country of origin. Once these conditions are satisfied, there is a good chance of finding something worthwhile.

### British metalwork
In the making of metal objects, as in all the other decorative arts of

the period, the influence of William Morris's Arts and Crafts movement and its theory of hand-working was strongly felt. However, as metal-work lends itself easily to machine production in the execution of good designs, machine techniques were used in England at a time when glass, ceramics and other media were still being worked in the new style by hand.

W. A. S. Benson (1854–1924) was associated with William Morris but broke away early to design metal objects that could be machine-produced. Most of his designs were for domestic and useful objects made of nickel, copper and brass, and his work inspired later designers in England like Llewellyn Rathbone and Arthur Dixon. Dixon designed for the Birmingham Guild of Handicrafts; many of his designs were executed in base metals, but he also designed articles in silver with semi-precious stones as decoration.

Silver, a material that the British have long been expert in designing and working, was used frequently by Art Nouveau designers and crafts-men, though their methods were somewhat different from the methods used before. Clement Heaton, Alexander Fisher, Phoebe Traquair and Harold Stabler all used enamel decoration on silver objects of their design. Cloisonné, a Chinese technique for the decoration of metal, was used during the Art Nouveau period by French designers and at least a couple of the British designers studied the technique of enamelling in France.

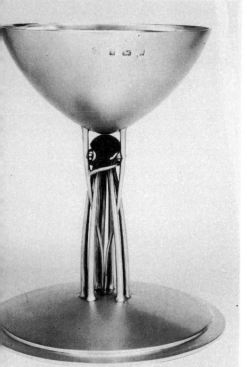

*(left) Silver cup designed for Liberty & Co by Archibald Knox, 1903. [John Jesse]; (below) Pewter centrepiece made for Liberty & Co, London. Marked: Tudric. [Marie Whitney Antiques]*

Many of the leading British metalworkers of the period designed for several different companies during their lifetimes; so it is extremely difficult, unless one is certain of the provenance of an item, to identify the designers conclusively. While the hallmark of a company is a clue to the date of a piece of British silver and the identity of the manufacturer, the designer often remains anonymous. In items made of the baser metals there is often no method of identification. The collector must trust his own instincts as to what is or is not good Art Nouveau design and buy accordingly. Signed items in metalwork, as in other materials, are more valuable than those that cannot be identified, and identification is always important in collecting, but the extra bonus of a signature is improbable on many Art Nouveau collectables, where the design might have been executed in a small workshop that will always remain anonymous. The unsigned piece, however, is often well worth owning. It may have been designed by an artist and made by a gifted craftsman who were not afraid of experimentation. Among the later mass-produced objects, those that required some hand-finishing are quite collectable. Liberty commissioned many decorative metal objects that were hand-finished or decorated by talented craftsmen. Silver boxes set with semi-precious stones or decorated with cloisonné are examples of metalwork that could be turned out by machine but had to be decorated by artists. Liberty merchandise was marked, but it is usually difficult to identify the artist who designed the piece or the man who decorated it.

For the fortunate collector who is able to find and afford articles made in England during the Art Nouveau period in silver, there is no better investment for future antique value. Because the British have always understood silver as a medium for decorative objects, the workmanship will be the best in the world and the quality of the silver the finest. Usually the design is excellent because inept designers are not often given the opportunity to work with very expensive materials. There is no serious problem in determining the age of Art Nouveau silver because the style lasted only a short time and English silver is hallmarked in any case. No one has yet begun to reproduce the Art Nouveau designs, though every other decorative style has been reproduced. While one must be an expert when purchasing silver made in other period styles to be certain that one is not buying a fake or reproduction, we need only be able to recognise good Art Nouveau design to be sure that a purchase is genuine. While the collector of English Art Nouveau silver may not see an enormous appreciation in value during his own lifetime, his heirs will admire his foresight.

Liberty commissioned many of the leading designers to design articles in Art Nouveau style, and they were then made in factories chosen by the firm. Pewter (with a high silver content) and silver articles were made. Almost all the designs required hand-finishing. Fireplace tools, fenders and andirons were made of iron. Decorative pieces were made in silver as well as the baser metals and these items include vases, boxes, dressing-table accessories, picture frames, plates and bowls.

## Belgium and France

The Belgian, Henry Van de Velde, who was trained as a painter and was caught up in the Art Nouveau movement, thereby turning his attention to crafts, designed objects in metal as well as other materials. His candlesticks, bowls and jewellery are decorated in the two-dimensional flat design that was in total harmony with the overall design of an object. Van de Velde believed that the material used should help determine the design, a revolutionary hypothesis for the time, and his influence can

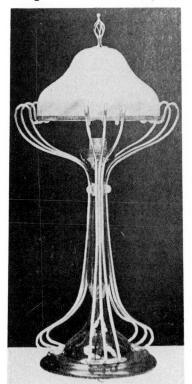

*(left) Lamp, silver and glass, British, designed by Harry Powell. [The Studio, 14 April, 1906]; (below) Pewter bowl, German. Marked: Kayserzinn. [Mr and Mrs Arthur Greenblatt]*

77

still be found in functional modern furniture and decoration. There is little of Van de Velde's work likely to come on the market today, but there appear, occasionally, later pieces that were influenced by his work that are highly collectable. Most of Van de Velde's known pieces of metalwork are already in museums.

Many of the French furniture designers and architects working in the new style also designed objects in metal. For one, they designed the hardware and decorative metal accessories for rooms to be furnished in the Art Nouveau style. The metal objects from France show the same rococo influences as the furniture of the Paris designers. Ormolu was used to decorate clock cases that were asymmetrical and had the flowing lines typical of French Art Nouveau. Inkstands can still be found that are nicely designed and executed. Often the designer and manufacturer are unidentifiable but it is not difficult for students and collectors of the period to ascertain the country of origin.

Like Van de Velde, the designers of Bing's group were versatile, so we have the architects and furniture designers making articles of many materials including metals for decorating rooms they had designed. The theory of the artists of the period that all things should be compatible in the new style led many of these men to see to every detail in their room designs. In contrast to the Arts and Crafts movement in England, much of the French Art Nouveau adapted nicely to the same sort of mass production that was used in England around the turn of the century, when the article was artist-designed, machine-made, and then finished or decorated by hand.

Towards 1900 the new art was at its height in France and everything that could be made in the plastic shapes and forms typical of the movement found a ready market. Some of these designs, naturally, were better than others. While there is still much to be collected, the buyer should be aware that he must trust his own judgement as to design and workmanship. Obviously, if the object in question is made of an important metal such as silver, ormolu or bronze it will have more intrinsic value. The success of the design in relation to the materials used is also an important factor. Some French Art Nouveau was badly designed and some was excellent. Naturally, pieces signed by known artists are of primary importance, but these are becoming more and more scarce and when available are usually very expensive. Even though France was not the leader in the Art Nouveau style as it had been in earlier decorative styles, the French interpretation of this style at its best will always be of value. The French made the most of the curvilinear line, the whiplash, the female figure and face and the organic flowing patterns that we have come to associate with Art Nouveau.

Georges de Feure was one of the French artists who worked most successfully in metal. His designs are more restrained than those of his contemporaries and his lamps and clocks are highly collectable. Lalique, famous for frosted and opalescent glass and his original jewellery designs, also designed silver objets d'art that were usually set with semi-precious stones.

## Germany and Austria

The German and Austrian designs were as different from the French as were the British. The Germans and Austrians adapted the rectilinear designs of the Secessionists rather than the undulating asymmetrical lines that were typically French. Geometrical shapes and decoration were used most often in German metalwork and these designs were quickly adapted for mass production.

Work was done in silver and pewter and one of the factories to turn out well designed pewter ware in the new style was Kayser Sohn, whose designers seemed to have had a better grasp of the ideas behind Art Nouveau than some others. Today, in comparison with other German metalwork of the period, the Kayser Sohn candlesticks and bowls made of pewter are distinctive because of the compatibility between the designs and the material used.

*Coal hod, German, steel, chrome-plated. No mark.*

 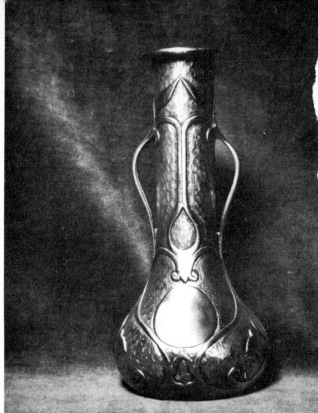

*(left) Lamp, bronze and glass, zodiac motifs on base. Marked: Tiffany Studios. [Dr and Mrs David Silvert]; (right) Silver bud vase, hand-embossed and chased. Probably American. No mark. [Dr and Mrs David Silvert]*

Kayser Sohn pewter is marked by the maker, and, therefore, easy to identify. It was exported to America and can sometimes be bought cheaply at estate auctions, since pewter collectors generally prefer earlier articles.

### America

Apart from the work done by Tiffany, there was little notable Art Nouveau metalwork made in the United States or now identifiable as truly American. As has been stated elsewhere in this book, the movement did not manifest itself in many areas of the applied arts in the United States until quite late. However, there were small groups of craftsmen and single designers who attempted to revive the art of hand-worked metal.

The most important of these groups was the Boston Society of Arts and Crafts, which gave its first exhibition in 1899 at Copley Hall. Their purpose was not to continue design in the manner of the European advocates of Art Nouveau. The 'American Art Annual' of 1916 holds Art Nouveau in disdain. In that volume, though hundreds of craftsmen are listed as working in the United States, the Secretary of the Society of Arts and Crafts of Boston states: 'I believe that the Arts and Crafts movement has reached a higher standard in the United States to-day (1916) than it has in England or on the Continent for the very reason that it has been broader and freer here. On the Continent it has been injured by the tendency toward the 'Art Nouveau' and in England it has been hampered also by socialist tendencies.'

By the time the arts and crafts of America had become a full-fledged movement, the Art Nouveau period was past its prime and some mass-produced articles were reflecting Art Nouveau designs at their worst. Therefore, the best of the style, with the exception of Tiffany and a few others, was to be passed over. The wealthy collectors of America were busy at the beginning of the century buying fine art and antiques in Europe, and it is not unlikely that some of them also bought examples of good American Art Nouveau, but the influence of these designs was negligible. The movement just got started too late to have been strongly influential in America and World War I put an end to its development completely.

Because the Arts and Crafts Movement had more importance in America than the Art Nouveau, there was experimentation with design

*Letter holder, pen tray and letter scale, grapevine pattern, silver on copper with blue opalescent glass set in. Marked: Tiffany Studios. Silver pen, ribbon design embossed. marked: Tiffany & Co.*

*Planter, brass with enamelled green finish. Amber glass panels set in. Insert has paper label reading: Murano, Patent, Aug. 1, 1906.*
[*Mr and Mrs Robert Belfit*]

by scattered designers and artisans. One problem in identifying some of the unsigned pieces of Art Nouveau style metal objects found in America is that a good deal of immigration was taking place at the turn of the century and workmen continued to work in their national styles once they arrived. If they experimented with designs, it would have been within the framework of what they had learned during their apprenticeships in their homelands. With so many craftsmen of different national origins working at the same time in America, it became impossible for a national style to develop.

For the above reasons, the American story of Art Nouveau in metalwork as well as glass must emphasise the work of Louis Comfort Tiffany. Although he was strongly influenced by work being done elsewhere, Tiffany's work was innovative and original in concept. Above all, he was conscious of the problems of mass production as opposed to handcrafting and in his metalwork he managed to combine both techniques successfully with excellent design.

For the collector of American applied arts of the period there is no doubt that the best investment is in signed Tiffany. It is difficult to discuss the work of Tiffany within the framework of one type of material, for much of his work in metal was in combination with glass. However, a discussion of his lamp bases is possible, for the designs are most typically Art Nouveau and often the beauty of some of the bronze work done by Tiffany's Studio is overshadowed by the beauty of the glass shades. Many of the lamp bases are fluid and organic in design and have motifs typical of Art Nouveau. The proportions are always absolutely correct in relation to the shade and the overall height and width of the lamp.

Tiffany Studio gift items in metal and glass, while reflecting the later mass-production efforts of the firm rather than the earlier hand-crafting, have become more popular in the past few years and, therefore, more expensive. The desk sets, boxes, bottles, etc, were designed originally as a means of using up scrap glass. Many of these items are made of metal filigree with iridescent or opalescent glass set behind it. The metal most often used was bronze, though there were many pieces made in silver plate or gilded metal. The most common combination is bronze with green iridescent glass.

Tiffany gift articles are still available for the collector, but caution should be observed when buying them: often the glass panels are cracked, a fault not easily discovered upon superficial inspection. Cracked or not, the prices of anything marked 'Tiffany Studios' keep soaring, nor have prices reached a peak. The demand for Tiffany items will always be strong, for there is little else American in the style that is as successful artistically.

While Tiffany lamps are presently beyond the reach of any but the richest collectors, 'wedding present Tiffany'—those boxes, desk sets and other items made to be given as gifts—are still within the reach of the average collector who wants to invest wisely in Art Nouveau.

*(left) Candlestick, bronze with twisted wire applied. American. Marked: M.W.T., Nov. 3, 1904. [Mr and Mrs Robert Belfit]; (right) Table lamp, American, bronze and glass, hand-painted. Marked: Handel. [Torrington Galleries]*

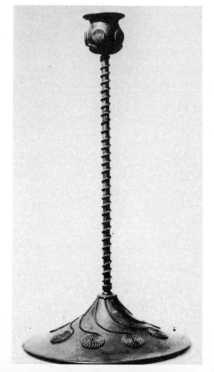 

# 9
# Posters

While most of the innovative theories and ideas in Art Nouveau originated in England, posters as an art form developed in France towards the close of the nineteenth century. The idea of coloured lithographed posters spread swiftly over the Continent, to England and thence to America, where this singular form of inexpensive advertising became established and grew in popularity. Each country's national style of Art Nouveau also dominated its style in posters. However, more than in any other medium, the talent and personality of single artists were of primary importance.

French Art Nouveau posters were influenced by the Japanese woodblock prints. The Japanese had long been using the poster form for advertising forthcoming productions in their theatres. The French interpretation of the Japanese poster style used brilliant colours, new to the art of lithography, and flourishing lines and patterns. Just as ornament in the new style for the home and person became the rage, ornament for the street took on new importance. The colourful addition of posters to urban scenery was approved by the French people, who gave posters the importance they have always given to good art.

The best posters were recognised as worthwhile from the beginning in France and were avidly collected. The heyday of the commercial poster in France began with the posters of Jules Cheret, Henri Toulouse-Lautrec and Théophile Steinlen. Eugène Grasset also worked in this medium with great success. These talented artists gave respectability to the idea of working in a practical form of art, one in which they could earn a living. Their posters advertised a variety of products, services, and coming events at the theatre.

Alphonse Mucha, whose association with Sarah Bernhardt led to the design of many unusual and effective posters, was an Hungarian artist

*Poster, Alphonse Mucha. [John Walters]*

working in Paris. His poster style has had a lasting effect on the entire Art Nouveau style. Pierre Bonnard, George Meunnier and many other artists turned from the fine arts to design posters that were fresh and original. However, the artists first mentioned created the poster style and for that reason their posters are the most sought after by collectors.

The British artists adapted poster art to their own more sombre temperaments. Frederick Walker designed the first British poster in 1871, to advertise Wilkie Collins' book, 'A Woman in White'. Curiously, this poster was in black and white and it is interesting that the black and white of Aubrey Beardsley followed soon after. Walter Crane

85

*Posters, Eugène Grasset.* [*John Walters*]

created more colourful posters as did R. Anning Bell, and the Macdonald
sisters and Herbert MacNair of the Glasgow Group also designed posters.
German posters signed P.K.S. (a group signature) were very effective
and are often seen today among poster collections. The poster art style
also spread quickly to Italy where the outstanding poster artists were
A. Hohenstein, Giuseppi Palanti and L. Metlicovitz. Railroads, hotels and
tourist agencies in Italy and Switzerland were quick to grasp the value
of artist-designed posters for advertising and this custom continues all
over the world.

In American poster art the names of Will Bradley and William Pen-
field stand out as innovators and work by both these men is highly
collectable. Much of Bradley's work was in black and white and many
of his posters were designed to advertise 'The Chap Book', Bradley's own
magazine. Although Bradley posters are much in demand by collectors,
the work of Frank Hazenplug, Claude Fayette Bragdon, J. J. Gould and
others is also worth collecting.

86

The above are but a few of the more innovative and important poster designers. There were many others who took up this new form of art around the turn of the century. The collector will find that the posters designed and signed by the recognised artists of the period are sometimes available but somewhat expensive. These posters are treated as important works of art, as well they should be. Occasionally, there are exhibits of Art Nouveau posters and even the less important posters have become collectors' items. Because the lithographed posters are somewhat fragile and were never meant to last, there are not too many of the good original Art Nouveau posters available. Obviously, those

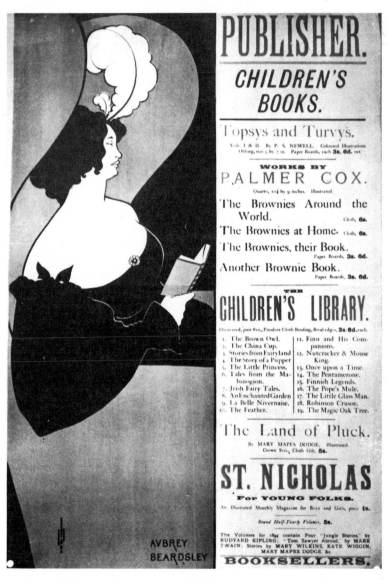

*Poster, Aubrey Beardsley. [John Walters]*

*Poster, Will Bradley. [John Walters]*

posters signed by recognised artists are valuable and are highly collect-able; they are also extremely decorative and for this reason they have long been in demand. Posters of lesser artists, with lettering and art style typical of the period, are also being collected now. The former, though expensive now, will probably increase in value; the latter are probably already overpriced.

With a renewed interest in the Art Nouveau style for interior decoration, many of the posters designed by Beardsley, Mucha, Bradley, Toulouse-Lautrec and others have recently been reprinted and are being used as decorative accessories for the home. Some have been seen for sale already matted and framed so that the copyright date is not visible. While this is not an attempt to sell these new prints as originals, it is not unlikely that as these posters become more popular some dealers will try to do so. The collector should be cautious, therefore, in future. It is always best to buy any work of art from a reputable gallery or art dealer. Remember that few unframed and unmounted posters have survived in their pristine condition, and that it is not difficult to age new prints.

# 10
# Books and Periodicals

For the collector of old and beautiful books the last quarter of the nineteenth century is one of the most interesting and most rewarding periods of printing, book design and illustration. In order to understand the historical, literary and artistic value of the books and periodicals important to this period, it is necessary once again to delve into the antecedents of Art Nouveau to find out what influences led to a revival of an art that had been almost totally neglected during the first three-quarters of the nineteenth century. This revival of interest in England in printing, book design and illustration finally was responsible for producing some of the most magnificent books the world was to see. Fortunately, the Art Nouveau influence in this area has been lasting.

Once again, when discussing the innovative aspects of Art Nouveau, it is necessary to give a large amount of credit to William Morris. Morris, involved in reviving an interest in all the crafts, was also a writer. It is not until he became dissatisfied with the appearance of the books he had written himself that he decided the arts of printing, illustration and bookbinding needed revival as much as did other forms of expression he had been advocating in his Arts and Crafts group. Morris's style of design imitated fifteenth-century manuscripts and reflected the page and print design of the Gothic style. However, his Kelmscott Press books did revive printing as an art form and quickly led to many reforms in book design. Printing, binding, illustrations and subject matter all came under close scrutiny of the artists working in other media. Much was found to be lacking. Once again, as in other media revived during the last half of the century, the art of printing and designing books demanded the attention of first rate artists and designers.

There had been, of course, isolated cases of artist-designed books before and during Morris's preoccupation with the Kelmscott Press.

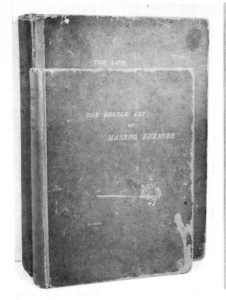

*(above left) Whistler's style of bookbinding, brown cover with yellow cloth spine, was later copied by his biographers, the Pennells; (above right) Illustration by Kay Nielson from* East of the Sun and West of the Moon *has elongated figure and stylised plants and flowers. Published by George H. Doran Company, New York, no date. [The Christmas Tree Bookshop]; (below) Whistler devised his own style of book design using stock print. Note wide outside margins and careful placement of annotations and the butterfly signatures.*

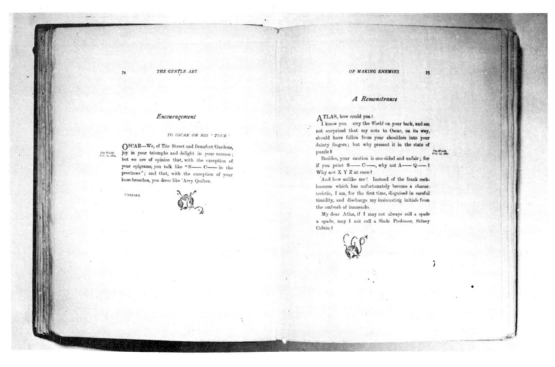

Dante Gabriel Rossetti designed bookbindings shortly after the middle of the century that herald the use of stylised floral forms as decorative motifs. Rossetti had been influenced by the work of William Blake, the artist and poet, who believed strongly in the total integration of writing and art. Blake illustrated and sometimes had his wife hand-colour his books of poetry.

Another great artist whose work had a strong influence on illustration and book design was James McNeill Whistler. Whistler did not illustrate his books, but included his butterfly signature in many forms as an expression of his attitudes in his writings. In his book about the famous Ruskin-Whistler trial, 'The Gentle Art of Making Enemies', Whistler worked closely with his printer in the choice of print, the placement of print on the page and the binding of the books. He chose a brown paper cover with a yellow cloth-covered spine. His title-pages were designed so that the print was off-centre. On the pages his print was placed unconventionally close to the centre of the book, with wide outside margins which he used for his fine-print annotations and butterflies. This book style had enormous influence in books that followed. It is interesting that his official biographers, the Pennells, chose the same binding style for their volumes of Whistler's life, as did T. R. Way when he published a list of Whistler's lithographs in 1896.

The Century Guild, which grew out of the Arts and Crafts movement, published a journal, 'The Hobby Horse', which shows Blake's influence and which integrated, in true Art Nouveau form, all the arts of the period. 'The Hobby Horse' was the first of many such journals, all of which are important in that they helped to spread the new style perhaps faster and more completely than any other method of communication at the time. A new print style in a new format on hand-made paper was used for this periodical. The moving force on the staff was Arthur H. Mackmurdo, who was a disciple of Morris and influenced in his art style by Whistler.

Another journal founded on the same principles as 'The Hobby Horse' was 'The Dial'. The first copy was issued in 1888 and Charles Ricketts was the artist-designer-writer responsible for its publication. Ricketts' art style showed the influences of Morris, Whistler and the Japanese woodblock artists, but he also borrowed from the style of the ancient Greeks and the fifteenth-century German wood-cut artists. From this eclectic mixture, Ricketts developed a non-literal style in the graphic arts—a style using black, white and grey planes and lines in the ethereal Art Nouveau mode.

*(above left) The black-and-white book illustration style spread to America early. This title page by George Wharton Edwards shows the use of the bold outline and little shading that was becoming popular in England. [The Christmas Tree Bookshop]; (above right) Cover of the book,* The Fairy Gifts and Tom Hickathrift. *Green cloth embossed in gold. [The Christmas Tree Bookshop]*

*Title page and illustration. The art nouveau style of illustration was extremely adaptable to children's books.*

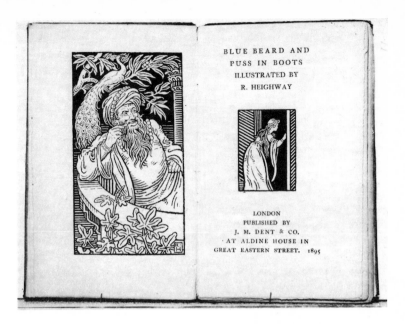

*Title page and illustration from* Blue Beard and Puss in Boots, *London, illustrated by R. Heighway.* [*The Christmas Tree Bookshop*]

Perhaps the first artist to design book illustrations that could be termed completely Art Nouveau in style was Aubrey Beardsley. He had full understanding of the value of working with black and white line blocks and he used the void in his compositions in a way that no other artist had yet attempted. Beardsley did illustrations for two periodicals or journals of the period, 'The Savoy' and 'The Yellow Book'. Editions of both of these journals have, in recent years, become collector's items, both for their value as rare books and as examples of influential art and literature of the period. Because they were both so totally aesthetic in concept and execution, they represent the ideals of Art Nouveau to perfection.

In France the art of book design was more the artist's province than the printer's. Toulouse-Lautrec designed lithographs to be used as book illustrations. Maurice Denis, a member of a group of young aesthetes called the 'Nabis', set about unifying the text with the illustrations; for previously there had been little unity in book printing and illustration, the one competing with the other rather than complementing it. Literal meaning was not as important as symbolic and emotional meaning, so Denis attempted a new concept of visual meaning in book illustration. He had been influenced by Gauguin and Seurat and his style shows those flat-planed languid lines that are Art Nouveau.

Word soon spread of the revival of the art of making books and of the integration of printing and illustrating. In France, where art has always

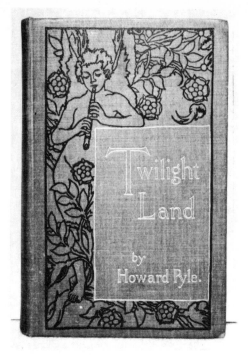

*(left) Cloth cover of* Twilight Land *was designed by the author, Howard Pyle, in 1903 and illustrates the use of bold outline and stylised plants popular at the beginning of the century. American. [The Christmas Tree Bookshop]; (right) Illustration from* Twilight Land *by Howard Pyle. Use of white space is reminiscent of Japanese prints and Whistler etchings.*

been of supreme importance, more and more good artists turned to the illustration of books and worked as enthusiastically as they did on exhibition paintings. Lithography and wood engraving were revived and the magnificent art books of this century are a direct result of the Art Nouveau movement, William Morris's Arts and Crafts, and the efforts of Burne-Jones, Mackmurdo, Charles Ricketts and others.

It is difficult to discuss books of the Art Nouveau period in the aspect of rare-book collecting. Book collecting as a hobby is a complicated field and the many facets of collectable books from this fertile period cannot be covered in one chapter or even in one volume. The criteria with which the bibliophile judges books to be rare and desirable have little to do with books of importance designed during the Art Nouveau period. Obviously, from the standpoint of the decorative arts the unusual and beautiful bindings of the period are of primary interest. Also of importance are the volumes that were illustrated by the leading artists of the period: Beardsley's illustrations for Oscar Wilde's 'Salome' are of interest to those of us enamoured of Beardsley's style; and the 1896 edition of 'The Rape of the Lock' might also be an exceptional find for the Beardsley enthusiast. These two volumes are less likely to be found today than copies of 'The Yellow Book' and the other journals of the period, which, while still available, become more expensive every year. The list of British Art Nouveau books that are collectable for their innovative bindings and illustrations is too long for the limitations of this chapter. The bindings designed by Charles Ricketts are works of art and worth owning for their beauty alone. There are hundreds of books published in England at the turn of the century and after that display magnificent bindings and illustrations in the Art Nouveau style. The period ushered in the revival of tooled and gilded leather bindings, metal clasps and spines and the use of unusual covering materials. The style was used for expensive limited editions as well as for inexpensive books issued in large quantities. Once a collector of Art Nouveau items is aware of the art styles and motifs used during the period he might possibly find among any quantity of books from the turn of the century one or two that typify the style of the period.

*(left) Periodical,* Lotus, *American, published by Japanese-American, Bunkio Matsuki, who was importer and dealer in Japanese art objects at turn of century; (right) Title page of magazine,* Lotus. *It is not known whether more issues followed this initial publication.*

# 11
# Where to find Art Nouveau Collectables

The sources for innovative, interesting items in Art Nouveau are some-what more abundant than are the sources for older articles in the field of the applied arts. Many fine objects, made by recognised artists or factories, are still in the hands of descendants of the original owners, but from time to time find their way to dealers or to auction houses. Those pieces that are signed, such as Tiffany or Gallé, are instantly recognised and, therefore, the collector will be in competition with the growing number of dealers who are handling Art Nouveau items more and more frequently as their sources for older decorative items dry up. For more esoteric items, the knowledgeable collector often has a fair chance to purchase Art Nouveau, sometimes at very low prices.

Bona-fide estate auctions, those that often include worthless house-hold effects, are perhaps the best sources for adding to one's collection. This type of auction often requires more time and patience than money and dealers in antiques cannot afford to spend the time when only one or two objects may interest them. Therefore, the collector armed with some knowledge of what is good design in the Art Nouveau style, can sometimes purchase the one or two collectable items that might have been wedding presents at the turn of the century. For the dedicated collector with more time than money this is the easiest and often the most rewarding method of finding things. Listings of this type of auction will often offer no clue as to what might be found in the inventory. A listing will often tell one that there are items of brass, glass or pottery, but unless these things are really old or signed with a recognisable mark they will not receive a separate listing and are sometimes tossed off by the auctioneer as being of little importance.

The finest auction houses in the world have all had auctions devoted

*Small colour print, Dutch.*
*Signed: Paul Berthon.*

solely to collections of Art Nouveau glass and furniture. So prices of Tiffany and Gallé glass have now settled at a very high level. However, good art glass is still available, and for the collector who must have a particular item, at any price, there is no real shortage as yet of Tiffany and Gallé. Antique dealers have been storing these things against the time when they would become desirable and owners are quite willing to part with their possessions once the market price is high enough. At the best auction houses the prices will be high, but the merchandise will be of fine quality. The collector usually has a choice of many different items of about the same age and made by the best firms. An auction catalogue for one of the leading auction houses may list as many as 100 Tiffany items, for instance, and the condition as well as the description and signature are catalogued. Unless the collector is certain of values and has had considerable auction experience, he would do well at this type of auction to ask his dealer to bid for him. This is particularly true at British auctions where the dealers will charge a small commission for buying an item for a client, who, in turn, has the advantage of the dealer's advice and knowledge and the authority he has with the auction house.

*Glove box, sold in unfinished state and decorated at home by American amateurs. This box signed and dated: Alice F. Heuer, Feb. 22, 1908. The design is carved to give the effect of curly maple, though the wood is pine.*

The excitement of finding good collectable items in out-of-the-way markets or secondhand shops is often the lure for collecting Art Nouveau. Perhaps this is the only category of collecting in the decorative arts where the possibility of finding something really worthwhile exists. This category takes in so many art forms that something worthwhile is likely to turn up quite frequently for the determined shopper. There is always the chance that a bookshop will have one or two of the beautifully illustrated and bound books of the period or that a piece of handsome hand-blown art glass will have escaped the attention of the dealers.

*French costume designs, watercolour. [John Walters]*

Those collectors with good eyesight and small pocketbooks can often find Art Nouveau jewellery that is of little value in materials but is of good design. There are still pieces of furniture made in Art Nouveau style that will be classified by the dealers as 'secondhand' rather than 'antique' and might, therefore, be inexpensive when found. Look for those things that have some evidence of hand-work and good design in the Art Nouveau style. A table with a good inlay is certainly worth rescuing from the junk heap. Bronze lamp bases and art glass shades are now of value whether they are marked 'Tiffany' or not. Bronze ink-wells, already an oddity to the 'now' generation, are quite collectable and there were many made of excellent Art Nouveau design.

The serious collector of Art Nouveau who is only interested in owning the best of the period should consider buying only from those dealers who specialise in the period. While there are not many of these dealers there are a few in the major cities of the world and it is usually into their hands that the very best collectable items of the period eventually come. A knowledgeable dealer who has a reputation for carrying only the very best in any category of collectable items is an invaluable aid to the serious collector. The dealer is quite willing to share knowledge gained from long years of study and he has sources for finding what the collector is searching for not available to the amateur. Specialist dealers will pay high prices for the very best and will guarantee the objects they sell both as to condition and, where possible, provenance.

*Jewel box, white metal, gilded. Design and decoration are totally integrated in this type of box, of which many were made after the turn of the century. [Mr and Mrs Arthur Greenblatt]*

*Silver picture frame, embossed. American. No mark. [Dr and Mrs David Silvert]*

The specialist dealer is the only method of purchase the collector should use when he is spending considerable sums. The dealer will also buy back items when the collector wishes to weed out or upgrade a collection. The leading dealers value their reputations and conduct their businesses accordingly. As good Art Nouveau items become scarce, the reputable dealers will become the only sources for the innovative, unusual, attributable items. The specialist dealer is as important to the collector as the collector is to him. Because there is not yet as much published information in the field of Art Nouveau applied arts as there is in older categories, the knowledge that the dealer has gathered over years of study is invaluable to the collector and also on occasions to museums, for which the specialist dealer frequently buys.

Once the collector has acquired enough knowledge he is apt to find collectable items wherever used or antique items for the home are sold. The collector who is able to recognise the value of the many collectable Art Nouveau items is often at an advantage with the dealer of general antique articles. Etchings of the period are sometimes sold for very little if a dealer is not aware of the artists of the period. Frequently an auctioneer will ask for the value of the frame if he has no knowledge of art. Lithographs, posters, carved or decorated boxes and other collectables are sometimes given little value because they are not truly 'antique'. The collector should know what is worth buying and must trust his own judgement if he is looking for true bargains.

# 12
# Conclusion

In the preceding chapters an attempt has been made to acquaint the collector and the would-be collector with the concepts of Art Nouveau and the products of the designers and artists working in that style and period. One important aspect of Art Nouveau design, architecture, has been omitted for obvious reasons. While important to the total picture of Art Nouveau, architecture is of little interest to collectors. It is important to remember, however, that many of the designers who were innovative in interior design were, first and foremost, architects; they designed furnishings that would complement their rooms.

It is impossible, within the confines of one volume, to represent all the work done in an extremely prolific period of the decorative arts. It is to be hoped that the collector has gained a feeling for those designs and motifs that are most representative of the period and that the repetition of certain motifs that were used in a decorative manner will aid the collector in recognising items that are similar to those illustrated here. The inclusion of some of the marks used on ceramics and glass should be of some help also. It must be remembered that the urge for expression in the arts and crafts spread to amateurs as well as the professional designers. It was the custom in the nineteenth century for ladies to occupy themselves with ceramic decoration and other do-it-yourself projects. Therefore, many hand-painted plates, vases and dishes may bear the mark of a recognised company and the signature of an amateur decorator. Limoges exported many blank china pieces for decoration in this manner to America; many of these items are charming and representative of the popular interpretations of the Art Nouveau style. There will be many other items that are obviously professional in quality but that cannot be identified as to the maker. If all other criteria point to the piece as being of good design and quality, this

*(left) Detail of art nouveau picture frame showing a departure from the heavy ornate style of the Victorian period; (right) Epergne, English, silver and glass. The art nouveau stylised flower form was adapted for many centrepieces, which were out of favour for a long time but are once more gaining in popularity with collectors. [Marie Whitney Antiques]*

should be no deterrent to the collector of Art Nouveau, though any collector tends to consider signed and recognised work to be of more value.

While most of the important collectable items fall into the categories of furniture, metalwork, glass, ceramics, books or posters, there are items made of other materials and in other forms that are important to the story of Art Nouveau design. Many of these were mass-produced when the style was at its height at the turn of the century.

Some of the items that can be found today are picture frames of wood or metal, boxes, printed fabrics, embroideries, etchings, lithographs and many other decorative items. If the motifs, patterns and lines are of the style and period they are probably worth buying, providing the collector likes them. There were many commercially made items, however, that were not particularly well designed in the first place, and they haven't improved with age.

As the supply of signed important pieces of art glass, ceramics, etc, decreases, the less important but comparably good pieces will become more desirable as collector's items. Also, as more research is done it is possible that many of these hitherto unidentifiable items will gain in stature in the field of the applied arts. Not many years ago all Art Nouveau was considered to be just 'fun' or 'camp'. Its revival raised the status of Tiffany glass and other similar decorative items, but it also raised the prices. Renewed interest in Art Nouveau has caused people to search their attics and basements for relics that they had meant to throw out years ago, and as these are studied and given attention through articles, books and museum studies, each object of good design will find its level as a collectable item. Good design and careful execution of that design, representative of the social, economic and artistic period in which it was done, always finds its proper place in the history of the decorative arts. The fortunate collector is the one who can see those qualities that make for good design before an item has been thoroughly researched.

Perhaps something should be said here about those collectable items that strongly influenced the entire Art Nouveau movement, the articles that were exported from Japan to the West during the latter half of the nineteenth century. Japanese ceramics lost much of their popularity during this century and it is only recently that they have been sought after by collectors. Japanese woodblock prints, which strongly influenced the arts, are just beginning to recover the attention they once enjoyed.

At present Art Nouveau is alive and hiding between the covers of almost every American and British magazine, on many printed fabrics, commercial packaging and in every wallpaper sample book. The undulating line smiles at us in the form of Toulouse-Lautrec-style lettering from billboards and posters and it is difficult to surmise what today's commercial artists would have done without the Art Nouveau style from which they have taken many of their ideas. Entire rooms are currently being decorated in what is known as 'Art Nouveau Style' with the most popular backgrounds being adaptations of black and white 'Beardsley' prints used with bright accents. This style has recently become so popular that wallpaper and fabrics are again being printed by Liberty of London from the original designs that once made that firm the style leader in home decoration.

Copies of Tiffany lampshades, made of plastic, a material of our own time, hang from the ceilings of hundreds of college dormitories whose occupants wear the tight Edwardian style of dress popular seventy years ago. These students date girls who look very much like Mucha's poster ladies with tendrils of flowing hair and pale skin. Posters designed in the same letter styles used at the turn of the century announce the details for next week's 'sit-in', 'be-in', or 'love-in'. Courses in ceramics and glassblowing have been added to college curriculums.

This kind of revival probably won't last. However, it has brought renewed attention to the strange movement in the decorative arts that began in the nineteenth century and it has made collectors, antique dealers and museums more aware of the real Art Nouveau. It has also accustomed an entire generation, including many future collectors, to an art style that was mostly ignored by their parents' generation. Obviously the younger generation accepts and likes this style and, therefore, it is not unlikely that as they learn something of the historical background of the Art Nouveau movement they will be grateful that some of us have collected and preserved the best of the period.

It is difficult to predict in what direction the decorative arts will go. There is an eclectic style popular at present in which furniture and accessories of all periods are successfully blended. Collecting for the home has never been more popular, for now it is not only the wealthy who can collect; often it is those who have a lot of knowledge and limited funds who find the best values in old accessories for home decoration. Art Nouveau design is at home on eighteenth-century desks

*(left) American adaptation of the shell form (in this case a real conch shell was used) for decorative use. Base is pewter. No mark; (right) Gold-plated bronze vase. Bird motif is simple and stylised. Marked: Siver Crest, S.H.A. Co. American.*

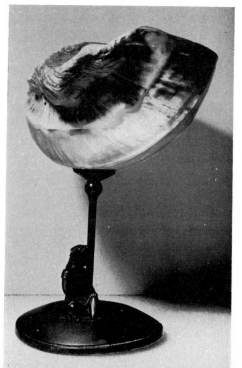

in the form of inkwells, letter openers, small decorative boxes and other items. Art glass collections are displayed in neo-classic cabinets.

The functional furniture that evolved after World War I was thought to have been completely new and original when it was first designed, but those who are aware of Morris's Arts and Crafts movement can see many similarities in the simplicity of style and colour and the use of hand-work that went into the early functional furniture designed in Germany. Art Nouveau style is the link between the centuries, and accessories of that period go well with the functional furnishings of today.

A direct outcome of the Art Nouveau movement is the revival of interest in handicrafts. Industry is once again taking a long look at its products and their design and is finally giving a freer rein to its designers and artists so that they may be able to develop new ideas without the usual pressure. Colleges are offering courses in handicrafts with emphasis on original design and workmanship. Industry often subsidises these courses because it knows full well that it must depend on the natural creative talent of artists for new ideas in design.

The theories of the Art Nouveau designers are being applied to newly developed materials and in some ways these theories adapt well to synthetics. Because the emphasis on design and innovative methods is so recent, but apes the ideas of the Art Nouveau designers, it is difficult to tell whether the effects this time will be lasting or not. However, it is no longer thought that the influence of the Art Nouveau philosophy and style was only passing. Good design will always be revived and used in new ways with new materials. The best of any decorative period is worth preserving. It is to be hoped that the collector of Art Nouveau will manage to save whatever is still available to him for the study of future generations.

At the beginning of this century, collecting in the decorative arts was considered a prerogative of the very rich, but an improved standard of living and mass education have brought about a phenomenon where, it seems, everyone collects something. In the age of collecting it is difficult to make any predictions concerning future values. We can only look to the past for information as to what has risen in price on the antiques market and judge today's collectable items by that.

Setting aside the category of fine arts, which is not really a concern of the collector of Art Nouveau applied arts, the one category that seems to increase enormously in value as time goes by is furniture. It is highly likely that artist-designed furniture in the Art Nouveau style,

*American ceramic-tile designers did not quite grasp the use of art nouveau motifs. These tiles are artistically unsuccessful, but amusing. Made in Ohio.*

particularly those pieces signed or otherwise attributable to the major artists, will be of enormous value once they become antiques. Certainly, a Majorelle table or sideboard is no longer considered to be 'used furniture' but is recognised as a major work of art and of importance in the history of the decorative arts. This is true, also, of those innovative pieces of furniture that incorporated several kinds of workmanship such as leather tooling, stained glass and marquetry in the Art Nouveau style. These items, and others of equal importance, have already become desirable and command high prices. However, when compared with furniture of other historically and artistically important periods, the prices are obviously nowhere near what they will be when the furniture is older. The hand-work in most of the pieces of Art Nouveau furniture cannot be duplicated today at any price. While it may not be within the average collector's means to buy these important items, there are smaller articles that are still relatively inexpensive; that is, that cost as much as a new piece of furniture of equal size and utility. These less important items in Art Nouveau will increase in value also.

Since it will be a while before Art Nouveau collectables become truly antique, it is important for the collector to buy and collect only that which has aesthetic appeal for him. Let the dealer purchase Art Nouveau for future investment. The collector must live with what he buys and should buy only what he enjoys looking at and living with. If you think an item beautiful or interesting and you know it to be of good design, chances are that when you or an heir decides to dispose of it, there will be someone else who will appreciate it also.

For some indication of the rising values of Art Nouveau items, we may look at the history of Tiffany glass and other innovative art glass of the period. Prices of art glass have doubled and tripled over the past fifteen years. If this is some indication of what may happen to other articles of the period, the Art Nouveau collector can look smugly upon his purchases. Innovative and original items are certain to increase in value. The degree to which prices rise will have to do with the state of the economy and the place that a particular item finds eventually in the history of the style.

Collectables of the Art Nouveau category are not yet considered antique. Neither are many of the things made during this period practical. These decorative but useless items are unique and, therefore, will not appeal to all collectors. Many collectors will find themselves specialising in one category or another. While the innovative ceramics of the period may appeal to some, others will buy only the art glass and many may specialise further in the work of one designer or maker. The Tiffany collector will scorn any other glass made during the period as inferior to what he desires and the collector of Gallé glass will defend his taste to the last, asserting that Tiffany is only an adaptation of that which Gallé made.

Those collectors who are interested in the history and development of, for instance, British pottery, will attempt to include examples of the innovative work done by the potters in the Art Nouveau period. The Wedgwood collector, if he is fortunate enough to be able to find it and afford it, will include a piece or two of fairyland lustre in his collection because it is representative of Wedgwood's interpretation of the art style that was so strongly influenced by the Japanese ceramics.

Those bibliophiles who are interested in excellent illustrations and unusual and beautiful bindings will search for and pay almost any price for rare books of the Art Nouveau period and collectors of prints and etchings will delight in finding examples of work by the artists of importance who were influenced by the style or who were, themselves, influential in spreading the style. The most prized possession of anyone who is enamoured of poster art will be a Mucha or Beardsley poster. Poster collecting has become a hobby for those who appreciate the work of first rate artists and yet who cannot afford to invest in original works of art. Since this medium began in the Art Nouveau period, these posters are certain to rise in value.

Because of the recent popularity of the Art Nouveau style, which, according to many, has been overdone by those responsible for wallpaper, fabric designs, letter styles in advertising, and magazine layouts and art work, it is possible that in another generation there will be some confusion concerning the genuineness of many of the collectable items designed in the style. It is also probable that interest in collecting Art Nouveau will temporarily wane. History has shown that when there is a strong revival of any style in the applied arts, this interest reaches a peak and then recedes. This may happen with Art Nouveau. However, history has also shown that when the imitations and copies have long been forgotten, that which was the best of the original period rises even higher in value than it did during the first revival. This has happened with items of the neo-classic period and there is little doubt that it will happen with many Art Nouveau collectables. The innovative artist-designed pieces have already reached the category of quality collectables and are currently being sold by the leading auction houses in the world, where the fact that they have been catalogued and priced keeps them from ever sliding back into anonymity. With a decline in the economy these items may not bring the same high prices, but they will forever be on record as having intrinsic monetary and artistic value.

Recognition by museums of a style or an item made or designed by a particular man or men will also ensure its future value even in a wavering money market. While museums in England, most particularly the Victoria and Albert in London, have long recognised the historic and artistic value to Great Britain of the Arts and Crafts and the Art Nouveau movements, it is still possible to find similar items to those which are on display on museum shelves. The British have attempted to preserve examples of the best work done during the period by their own countrymen and artists of other countries. The acceptance of a gift or a purchase by a major museum raises the artistic value and also the monetary value of another piece that is similar, identical or executed or designed by the same artist.

The truly dedicated collector will buy that which he likes regardless of possible increase in value. If he is fortunate enough to be able to find the excellent articles that were made during the Art Nouveau period, he can rest assured that, while he enjoys the pleasure of living with good design and examples of excellent craftsmanship, as his collection grows older it will also become more valuable.

# Bibliography

Bland, David. 'The Illustration of Books', London (1962)

Champney, Freeman. 'Art and Glory: The Story of Elbert Hubbard', New York (1968)

Cox, Warren E. 'The Book of Pottery and Porcelain', Volume II, New York (1944)

Drexler, Arthur and Daniel, Greta. 'Introduction to Twentieth Century Design from the Collection of the Museum of Modern Art', Garden City (1959)

Eberlin, Harold D. and Ramsdell, Roger W. 'The Practical Book of Chinaware', Philadelphia and New York (1948)

Freeman, John Crosby. 'Antiques Furniture Handbook': Volume 5, 'Mission and Art Nouveau', Watkins Glen (1966)

Godden, Geoffrey A. 'Encylopaedia of British Pottery and Porcelain Marks', New York (1964)

Grover, Ray and Lee. 'Art Glass Nouveau', Rutland (1967)

Hartmann, Sadakichi. 'Japanese Art', Boston (1904)

Hayward, Helena (editor). 'World Furniture—an Illustrated History', New York-Toronto (1965)

Henderson, James. 'Silver Collecting for Amateurs', New York (1968)

Jones, E. Alfred. 'Old Silver of Europe and America From Early Times to the Nineteenth Century', Philadelphia (1928)

Koch, Robert. 'Louis C. Tiffany: Rebel in Glass', New York (1964)

Levy, Florence N. 'American Art Annual', Volume XI, New York (1914)

Lichten, Frances, 'Decorative Arts of Victoria's Era', New York (1950)

Madsen, S. Tschudi. 'Art Nouveau', New York (1967)

Matsuki, Bunkio. 'Lotus', Volume I, Number I, Boston (1903)

Menpes, Mortimer. 'Whistler as I Knew Him', London (1904)

Ormsbee, Thomas H. 'Care and Repair of Antiques', New York (1954)

Price, Charles Matlack. 'Poster Design, A Critical Study of the Poster in Continental Europe, England and America', New York (1922)

Reade, Brian. 'Art Nouveau and Alphonse Mucha', London (1967)

Reade, Brian. 'Aubrey Beardsley', London (1966)

Rheims, Maurice. 'The Flowering of Art Nouveau', New York (1966)

Rickards, Maurice. 'Posters at the Turn of the Century', London (1968)

Rogers, Frances and Beard, Alice. 'Five Thousand Years of Gems and Jewelry', New York (1940)

Schmutzler, Robert. 'Art Nouveau', New York (1964)

Selz, Peter and Constantin, Mildred. 'Art Nouveau—Art and Design at the Turn of the Century', New York (1960)

Stirling, A. M. W. 'William De Morgan and his Wife', London (1922)

Strange, Edward F. 'Colour Prints of Japan—an Appreciation and History', London (1906)

Taylor, John Russell. 'The Art Nouveau Book in Britain', Amsterdam and London (1967)

'Tiffany and Other Art Glass, Art Nouveau and Bauhaus Furniture', Parke-Bernet Galleries, New York (1967)

Van Tassell, Valentine. 'Emile Gallé's Art Glass', 'The Antiques Journal', (June 1952)

Van Tassell, Valentine. 'Louis Comfort Tiffany', 'The Antiques Journal', (July and August 1952)

Van Tassell, Valentine. 'Thomas Webb's Butterflies', 'The Antiques Journal', (March 1952)

Victoria and Albert Museum. 'Catalogue of Exhibition of Victorian and Edwardian Decorative Arts', London (1952)

Victoria and Albert Museum. 'William Morris' (Small Picture Book, # 43), London (1958)

# Index